Forgotten

FREE BOOKS

www.*forgottenbooks*.org

You can read literally <u>thousands</u> of books
for free at www.forgottenbooks.org

(please support us by visiting our web site)

Truth may seem, but cannot be:
Beauty brag, but 'tis not she;
Truth and beauty buried be.

To this urn let those repair
That are either true or fair;
For these dead birds sigh a prayer.

Bacon

THE HARTFORD-LAMSON LECTURES ON THE RELIGIONS OF THE WORLD

VOLUME I

AN INTRODUCTION TO THE STUDY OF COMPARATIVE RELIGION

THE MACMILLAN COMPANY
NEW YORK · BOSTON · CHICAGO
ATLANTA · SAN FRANCISCO

MACMILLAN & CO., LIMITED
LONDON · BOMBAY · CALCUTTA
MELBOURNE

THE MACMILLAN CO. OF CANADA, LTD.
TORONTO

THE HARTFORD-LAMSON LECTURES ON
THE RELIGIONS OF THE WORLD

AN INTRODUCTION

TO THE STUDY OF

COMPARATIVE RELIGION

BY

FRANK BYRON JEVONS

PRINCIPAL OF BISHOP HATFIELD'S HALL, DURHAM
UNIVERSITY, DURHAM, ENGLAND

New York

THE MACMILLAN COMPANY

1908

NOTE

THE Hartford-Lamson Lectures on "The Religions of the World" are delivered at Hartford Theological Seminary in connection with the Lamson Fund, which was established by a group of friends in honor of the late Charles M. Lamson, D.D., sometime President of the American Board of Commissioners for Foreign Missions, to assist in preparing students for the foreign missionary field. The Lectures are designed primarily to give to such students a good knowledge of the religious history, beliefs, and customs of the peoples among whom they expect to labor. As they are delivered by scholars of the first rank, who are authorities in their respective fields, it is expected that in published form they will prove to be of value to students generally.

CONTENTS

ANALYTICAL TABLE OF CONTENTS

INTRODUCTION

The use of any science lies in its application to practical purposes. For Christianity, the use of the science of religion consists in applying it to show that Christianity is the highest manifestation of the religious spirit. To make this use of the science of religion, we must fully and frankly accept the facts it furnishes, and must recognise that others are at liberty to use them for any opposite purpose. But we must also insist that the science of religion is limited to the establishment of facts and is excluded from passing judgment on the religious value of those facts. The science of religion as a historical science is concerned with the chronological order, and not with the religious value, of its facts; and the order of those facts does not determine their value any more in the case of religion than in the case of literature or art. But if their value is a question on which the science refuses to enter, it does not follow that the question is one which does not admit of a truthful answer: science has no monopoly of truth. The value of anything always implies a reference to the future: to be of value a thing must be of use for some purpose, and what is purposed is in the future. Things have value, or have not, according as they are useful or not for our purposes. The conviction that we can attain our purposes and ideals, the conviction without which we should not even attempt to attain them is faith; and it is in faith and by faith that the man of religion proposes to

IMMORTALITY

The belief in immortality is more prominent, though less intimately bound up with religion, amongst uncivilised than it is amongst civilised peoples. In early times the fancy luxuriates, unchecked, on this as on other matters. It is late in the history of religion that the immortality of the soul is found to be postulated alike by morality and religion. The belief that the soul exists after death doubtless manifested itself first in the fact that men dream of those who have died. But, were there no desire to believe, it may be doubted whether the belief would survive, or even originate. The belief originates in desire, in longing for one loved and lost; and dreams are not the cause of that desire, though they are one region in which it manifests itself, or rather one mode of its manifestation. The desire is for continued communion; and its gratification is found in a spiritual communion. Such communion also is believed to unite worshippers both with one another and with their God. Where death is regarded as a disruption of communion between the living and the departed, death is regarded as unnatural, as a violation of the original design of things, which calls for explanation; and the explanation is provided in myths which account for it by showing that the origin of death was due to accident or mistake. At first, it is felt that the mistake cannot be one without remedy: the deceased is invited "to come to us again." If he does not return in his old body, then he is believed to reappear in some new-born child. Or the doctrine of rebirth may be satisfied by the belief that the soul is reincarnated in animal form. This belief is specially likely to grow up where totem ancestors are believed to manifest themselves in the shape of some animal. Belief in such animal reincarnation has, in its origin, however, no connection with any theory that transmigration from a human to an animal form is a punishment. Up to this point in the evolution of the belief in immortality, the belief in another world than this does not show itself. Even when ancestor-worship begins to grow up, the ancestors' field of operations is in this world, rather than in the next. But the fact that their aid and protection can be invoked by the community tends to elevate them to the level of the god or gods of the community. This tendency, however, may be defeated, as it was in Judæa, where the religious sentiment will not permit the difference between God and man to be blurred.

MAGIC

A view sometime held was that magic is religion, and religion magic. With equal reason, or want of reason, it might be held that magic was science, and science magic.

ANALYTICAL TABLE OF CONTENTS

Even if we correct the definition, and say that to us magic appears, in one aspect, as a spurious system of science; and, in another, as a spurious system of religion; we still have to note that, for those who believed in it, it could not have been a spurious system, whether of science or religion. Primitive man acts on the assumption that he can produce like by means of like; and about that assumption there is no "magic" of any kind. It is only when an effect thus produced is a thing not commonly done and not generally approved of, that it is regarded as magic; and it is magic, because not every one knows how to do it, or not every one has the power to do it, or not every one cares to do it. About this belief, so long as every one entertains it, there is nothing spurious. When however it begins to be suspected that the magician has not the power to do what he professes, his profession tends to become fraudulent and his belief spurious. On the other hand, a thing commonly done and generally approved of is not regarded as magical merely because the effect resembles the cause, and like is in this instance produced by like. Magic is a term of evil connotation; and the practice of using like to produce like is condemned when and because it is employed for anti-social purposes. Such practices are resented by the society, amongst whom and on whom they are employed; and they are offensive to the God who looks after the interests of the community. In fine, the object and purpose of the practice determines the attitude of the community towards the practice: if the object is anti-social, the practice is nefarious; and the witch, if "smelled out," is killed. The person who is willing to undertake such nefarious proceedings comes to be credited with a nefarious personality, that is to say, with both the power and the will to do what ordinary, decent members of the community could not and would not do: personal power comes to be the most important, because the most mysterious, characteristic of the man believed to

FETICHISM

Fetichism is regarded by some as a stage of religious development, or as the form of religion found amongst men at the lowest stage of development known to us. From this the conclusion is sometimes drawn that fetichism is the source of all religion and of all religious values; and, therefore, that (as fetichism has no value) religion (which is an evolved form of fetichism) has no value either. This conclusion is then believed to be proved by the science of religion. In fact, however, students of the science of religion disclaim this conclusion and rightly assert that the science does not undertake to prove anything as to the truth or the value of religion.

Much confusion prevails as to what fetichism is; and the confusion is primarily due to Bosman. He confuses, while the science of religion distinguishes between, animal gods and fetiches. He asserts what we now know to be false, viz., that a fetich is an inanimate object and nothing more; and that the native rejects, or "breaks," one of these gods, knowing it to be a god.

Any small object which happens to arrest the attention of a negro, when he has a desire to gratify, may impress him as being a fetich, *i.e.* as having power to help him to gratify his desire. Here, Höffding says, is the simplest conceivable construction of religious ideas: here is presented religion under the guise of desire. Let it be granted, then, that the object attracts attention and is involuntarily associated with the possibility of attaining the desired end. It follows that, as in the period of animism, all objects are believed to be animated by spirits, fetich objects are distinguished from other objects by the fact — not that they are animated by spirits but — that it is believed they will aid in the accomplishment of the desired end. The picking up of a fetich object, however, is not always followed by the desired result; and the negro then explains "that it has lost its spirit." The spirit goes out of it, indeed, but may perchance be induced or even compelled to return into some other object; and then fetiches may be purposely made as well as accidentally found, and are liable to coercion as well as open to conciliation.

But, throughout this process, there is no religion. Religion is the worship of the gods of a community by the community for the good of the community. The cult of a fetich is conducted by an individual for his private ends; and the most important function of a fetich is to work evil against those members of the community who have incurred the fetich owner's resentment. Thus religion

PRAYER

the moment the question is put, Whose desire? that of the individual or of the community? And instances may be cited to show that it is not for his own personal, selfish advantage alone that the savage always or even usually prays. It is the desires of the community that the god of the community is concerned to grant: the petition of an individual is offered and harkened to only so far as it is not prejudicial to the interests of the community. The statement that savage prayer is unethical may be correct in the sense that pardon for moral sin is not sought; it is incorrect, if understood to mean that the savage does not pray to do the things which his morality makes it incumbent on him to do, e.g. to fight successfully. The desires which the god is prayed to grant are ordinarily desires which, being felt by each and every member of the community, are the desires of the community, as such, and not of any one member exclusively.

Charms, it has been suggested, in some cases are prayers that by vain repetition have lost their religious significance and become mere spells. And similarly it has been suggested that out of mere spells prayer may have been evolved. But, on the hypothesis that a spell is something in which no religion is, it is clear that out of it no religion can come; while if prayer, i.e. religion, has been evolved out of spells, then there have never been spells wholly wanting in every religious element. Whether a given formula then is prayer or spell may be difficult to decide, when it has some features which seem to be magical and others which seem to be religious. The magical element may have been original and be in process of disappearing before the dawn of the religious spirit. Now, the formula uttered is usually accompanied by gestures performed. If the words are uttered to explain the gesture or rite, the explanation is offered to some one, the words are of the nature of a prayer to some one to grant the desire which the gesture manifests.

SACRIFICE

Prayer and sacrifice historically go together, and logically are indissoluble. Sacrifice, whether realised in an offering dedicated or in a sacrificial meal, is prompted by the worshippers' desire to feel that they are at one with the spirit worshipped. That desire manifests itself specially on certain regularly occurring occasions (harvest, seed time, initiation) and also in times of crisis. At harvest time the sacrifices or offerings are thank-offerings, as is shown by the fact that a formula of thanksgiving is employed. Primitive prayer does not consist solely in petitions for favours to come; it includes thanksgiving for blessings received. Such thanksgivings cannot by any possibility be twisted into magic.

Analogous to these thanksgivings at harvest time is the solemn eating of first-fruits amongst the Australian black fellows. If this solemn eating is not in Australia a survival of a sacramental meal, in which the god and his worshippers were partakers, it must be merely a ceremony whereby the food, which until it is eaten is taboo, is "desacralised." But, as a matter of fact, such food is not taboo to the tribe generally; and the object of the solemn eating cannot be to remove the taboo and desacralise the food for the tribe.

If the harvest rites or first-fruit ceremonials are sacrificial in nature, then the presumption is that so, too, are the ceremonies performed at seed time or the analogous period.

At initiation ceremonies or mysteries, even amongst the Australian black fellows, there is evidence to show that prayer is offered; and generally speaking we may say that the boy initiated is admitted to the worship of the tribal gods.

The spring and harvest customs are closely allied to one another and may be arranged in four groups: (1) In Mexico they plainly consist of the worship of a god — by means of sacrifice and prayer — and of communion.

(2) In some other cases, though the god has no proper or personal name, and no image is made of him, "the new corn," Dr. Frazer says, "is itself eaten sacramentally, that is, as the body of the corn spirit"; and it is by this sacramental meal that communion is effected or maintained. (3) In the harvest customs of northern Europe, bread and dumplings are made and eaten sacramentally, "as a substitute for the real flesh of the divine being"; or an animal is slain and its flesh and blood are partaken of. (4) Amongst the Australian tribes there is a sacramental eating of the totem animal or plant. Now, these four groups of customs may be all religious (and Dr. Frazer speaks of them all as sacramental) or all magical; or it may be admitted that the first three are religious, and maintained that the fourth is strictly magical. But such a separation of the Australian group from the rest does not commend itself as likely; further, it overlooks the fact that it is at the period analogous to harvest time that the headman eats solemnly and sparingly of the plant or animal, and that at harvest time it is too late to work magic to cause the plant or animal to grow. The probability is, then, that both the Australian group and the others are sacrificial rites and are religious.

Such sacrificial rites, however, though felt to be the means whereby communion was effected and maintained between the god and his worshippers, may come to be interpreted as the making of gifts to the god, as the means of purchasing his favour, or as a full discharge of their obligations. When so interpreted they will be denounced by true religion. But though it be admitted that the sacrificial rite might be made to bear this aspect, it does not follow, as is sometimes supposed, that it was from the outset incapable of bearing any other. On the contrary, it was, from the beginning, not only the rite of making offerings to the god but, also, the rite whereby communion was attained, whereby the society of worshippers was brought into the presence of the god they

MORALITY

The question whether morality is based on religion, or religion on morality, is one which calls for discussion, inasmuch as it is apt to proceed on a mistaken view of facts in the history of religion. It is maintained that as a matter of history morality came first and religion afterwards; and that as a matter of philosophy religion presupposes morality. Reality, that is to say, is in the making; the spirit of man is self-realising; being is in process of becoming rationalised and moralised; religion in process of disappearing.

Early religion, it is said, is unethical: it has to do with spirits, which, as such, are not concerned with morality; with gods which are not ethical or ideal, and are not objects of worship in our sense of the term.

Now, the spirits which, in the period of animism, are believed to animate things, are not, it is true, concerned with morality; but then, neither are they gods. To be a god a spirit must have a community of worshippers; and it is as the protector of that community that he is worshipped. He protects the community against any individual member who violates the custom of the community. The custom of the community constitutes the morality of the society. Offences against that custom are offences against the god of the community. A god starts as an ethical power, and as an object of worship.

Still, it may be argued, before gods were, before religion was evolved, morality was; and this may be shown by the origin and nature of justice, which throughout is entirely independent of religion and religious considera-

tions.   On this theory, the origin of justice is to be found
in the resentment of the individual.   But, first, the individual, apart from society, is an abstraction and an
impossibility: the individual never exists apart from
but always as a member of some society.   Next, justice
is not the resentment of any individual, but the sentiment of the community, expressing itself in the action not
of any individual but of the community as such.   The
responsibility both for the wrong done and for righting it
rests with the community.   The earliest offences against
which public action is taken are said to be witchcraft and
breaches of the marriage laws.   The latter are not in-
juries resented by any individual: they are offences
against the gods and are punished to avert the misfortunes which otherwise would visit the tribe.   Witchcraft is especially offensive to the god of the community.
In almost, if not quite, the lowest stages of human development, disease and famine are regarded as punishments
which fall on the community as a whole, because the
community, in the person of one of its members, has
offended some supernatural power.   In quite the lowest
stage the guilt of the offending member is also regarded
as capable of infecting the whole community; and he
is, accordingly, avoided by the whole community and
tabooed.   Taboo is due to the collective action, and expresses the collective feeling of the community as a
whole.   It is from such collective action and feeling that
justice has been evolved and not from individual resentment, which is still and always was something different
from justice.   The offences punished by the community
have always been considered, so far as they are offences
against morality, to be offences against the gods of the
community.   The fact that in course of time such offences
come to be punished always as militating against the
good of society testifies merely to the general assumption
that the good of man is the will of God: men do not
believe that murder, adultery, etc., are merely offences

CHRISTIANITY

the end is not yet. It is an end in which, whenever and if ever realised on earth, we who are now living shall not live to partake: we are — on this theory of the evolution of humanity — means, and solely means, to an end which, when realised, we shall not partake in. Being an end in which we cannot participate, it is not an end which can be rationally set up for us to strive to attain. Nor will the generation, which is ultimately to enjoy it, find much satisfaction in reflecting that their enjoyment has been purchased at the cost of others. To treat a minority of individuals as the end for which humanity is evolved, and the majority as merely means, is a strange pass for humanitarianism to come to.

Approaching the evolution of religion from the point of view that the individual must always be regarded both as an end and as a means, we find that Buddhism denies the individual to be either the one or the other, for his very existence is an illusion, and an illusion which must be dispelled, in order that he may cease from an existence which it is an illusion to imagine that he possesses. If, however, we turn to other religions less highly developed than Buddhism, we find that, in all, the existence of the individual as well as of the god of the community is assumed; that the interests of the community are the will of the community's god; that the interests of the community are higher than the interests of the individual, when they appear to differ; and that the man who prefers the interests of the community to his own is regarded as the higher type of man. In fine, the individual, from this point of view, acts voluntarily as the means whereby the end of society may be realised. And, in so acting, he testifies to his conviction that he will thereby realise his own end.

Throughout the history of religion these two facts are implied: first, the existence of the individual as a member of society seeking communion with God; next, the existence of society as a means of which the individual is

INTRODUCTION

Of the many things that fill a visitor from the old country with admiration, on his first visit to the United States, that which arrests his attention most frequently, is the extent and success with which science is applied to practical purposes. And it is beginning to dawn upon me that in the United States it is not only pure science which is thus practically applied, — the pure sciences of mechanics, physics, mathematics, — but that the historic sciences also are expected to justify themselves by their practical application; and that amongst the historic sciences not even the science of religion is exempted from the common lot. It also may be useful; and had better be so, — if any one is to have any use for it. It must make itself useful to the man who has practical need of its results and wishes to apply them — the missionary. He it is who, for the practical purposes of the work to which he is called, requires an applied science of religion; and Hartford Theological Seminary may, I believe, justly claim to be the first institution in the world which has deliberately and consciously set to work to create by the courses of lectures, of which this series is the very humble beginning, an applied science of religion.

How, then, will the applied science differ from the pure science of religion? In one way it will not differ: an applied science does not sit in judgment upon the pure science on which it is based; it accepts the truths which the pure science presents to all the world, and bases itself upon them. The business of pure science is to discover facts; that of the applied science is to use them. The business of the science of religion is to discover all the facts necessary if we are to understand the growth and history of religion. The business of the applied science is, in our case, to use the discovered facts as a means of showing that Christianity is the highest manifestation of the religious spirit.

In dealing with the applied science, then, we recover a liberty which the pure science does not enjoy. The science of religion is a historic science. Its student looks back upon the past;

and looks back upon it with a single purpose, that of discovering what, as a matter of fact, did happen, what was the order in which the events occurred. In so looking back he may, and does, see many things which he could wish had not occurred; but he has no power to alter them; he has no choice but to record them; and his duty, his single duty, is to ascertain the historic facts and to establish the historic truth. With the applied science the case is very different. There the student sets his face to the future, no longer to the past. The truths of pure science are the weapons placed in his hand with which he is to conquer the world. It is in the faith that the armour provided him by science is sure and will not fail him that he addresses himself to his chosen work. The implements are set in his hands. The liberty is his to employ them for what end he will. That liberty is a consequence of the fact that the student's object no longer is to ascertain the past, but to make the future.

The business of the pure science is to ascertain the facts and state the truth. To what use the facts and truth are afterwards put, is a question with which the pure science has nothing to do.

The same facts may be put to very different uses: from the same facts very different conclusions may be drawn. The facts which the science of religion establishes may be used and are used for different and for contradictory purposes. The man who is agnostic or atheist uses them to support his atheism or agnosticism; or even, if he is so unwise, to prove it. The man who has religion is equally at liberty to use them in his support; and if he rarely does that, at any rate he still more rarely commits the mistake of imagining that the science of religion proves the truth of his particular views on the subject of religion. Indeed, his tendency is rather in the opposite direction: he is unreasonably uneasy and apt to have a disquieting alarm lest the science of religion may really be a danger to religion. This alarm may very naturally arise when he discovers that to the scientific student one religion is as another, and the question is indifferent whether there is any truth in any form. It is very easy to jump from these facts to the erroneous conclusion that science of religion is wholly incompatible with religious belief. And of course it is quite human and perfectly intelligible that that conclusion should be proclaimed aloud as correct and inevitable by the man who, being an atheist, fights for what he feels to be the truth.

We must, therefore, once more insist upon the simple fact that science of religion abstains necessarily from assuming either that religion is true or is not true. What it does assume is what no one will deny, viz. that religion is a fact. Religious beliefs may be right or they may be wrong: but they exist. Therefore they can be studied, described, classified, placed in order of development, and treated as a branch of sociology and as one department of the evolution of the world. And all this can be done without once asking the question whether religious belief is true and right and good, or not., Whether it is pronounced true or false by you or me, will not in the least shake the fact that it has existed for thousands of years, that it has had a history during that period, and that that history may be written. We may have doubts whether the institution of private property is a good thing, or whether barter and exchange are desirable proceedings. But we shall not doubt that private property exists or that it may be exchanged. And we shall not imagine that the science of political economy, which deals, among other things with the production and exchange of wealth which is private property, makes any pronouncement whatever on the question whether private property is or is not an institution which we ought to support and believe in. The conclusions established by the science of political economy are set forth before the whole world; and men may use them for what purpose they will. They may and do draw very different inferences from them, even contradictory inferences. But if they do, it is because they use them for different ends or contradictory purposes. And the fact that the communist or socialist uses political economy to support his views no more proves that socialism is the logical consequence of political economy than the fact that the atheist uses or misuses, for his own purposes, the conclusions of the science of religion proves his inferences to be the logical outcome of the science.

The science of religion deals essentially with the one fact that religion has existed and does exist. It is from that fact that the missionary will start; and it is with men who do not question the fact that he will have to do. The science of religion seeks to trace the historic growth, the evolution of religion; to establish what actually was, not to judge what ought to have been, — science knows no "ought," in that sense or rather in that tense, the past tense. Its work is done, its last word has been said, when it has demonstrated what was. It is the heart which sighs to think what might have been, and which puts on it a higher value than it does on what actually came to pass. There is then another order in which facts may be ranged besides the chronological order in which historically they occurred; and that is the order of their value. It is an order in which we do range facts, whenever we criticise them. It is the order in which we range them, whenever we pass judgment on them. Or, rather, passing judgment on them is placing them in the order of their value. And the chronological order of their occurrence is quite a different thing from the order in which we rank them when we judge them according to their value and importance. It is, or rather it would be, quite absurd to say, in the case of literature, or art, for instance, that the two orders are identical. There it is obvious and universally admitted that one period may reach a higher level than another which in point of time is later. The classical period is followed by a post-classical period; culmination is followed by decline.

Now, this difference in point of the literary or artistic value of two periods is as real and as fundamental as the time order or chronological relation of the two periods. It would be patently ridiculous for any ardent maintainer of the importance of distinguishing between good literature and bad, good art and bad art, to say that the one period, being good, must have been chronologically prior to the other, because, from the point of art, it was better than that other. Every one can see that. The chronological order, the historic order, is one thing; the order of literary value or artistic importance is another. But if this is granted, and every one will grant it, then it is also, and thereby, granted that the historic order of events is not the same thing as the order of their value, and is no guide to it.

Thus far I have illustrated these remarks by reference to literary and artistic values. But I need hardly say that I have been thinking really all the time of religious values. If the student of literature or of art surveys the history of art and literature with the purpose of judging the value of the works produced, the student of religion may and must survey the history of religion with the same purpose. If the one student is entitled, as he justly is entitled, to say that the difference between the literary or artistic value of two periods is as real and as fundamental as is their difference in the order of time, then the student of religion is claiming no exceptional or suspicious privilege for himself. He is claiming no privilege at all; he is but exercising the common rights of all students like himself, when he points out that differences in religious values are just as real and just as fundamental as the historic or chronological order itself.

The assignment of values, then, — be it the assignment of the value of works of art, literature, or religion, — is a proceeding which is not only possible (as will be somewhat contemptuously admitted by those who believe that evolution is progress, and that there is no order of value distinct from the order of history and chronological succession) ; the assignment of value is not only permissible (as may be admitted by those who believe, or for want of thought fancy they believe, that the historic order of events is the only order which can really exist), it is absolutely inevitable. It is the concomitant or rather an integral part of every act of perception. Everything that we perceive is either dismissed from attention because it is judged at the moment to have no value, or, if it has value, attention is concentrated upon it.

From this point of view, then, it should be clear that there is some deficiency in such a science as the science of religion, which, by the very conditions that determine its existence, is precluded from ever raising the question of the value of any of the religions with which it deals. Why does it voluntarily, deliberately, and of its own accord, rigidly exclude the question whether religions have any value — whether religion itself has any value? One answer there is to that question which once would have been accepted as conclusive, viz. that the object of science is truth. That answer delicately implies that whether religion has any value is an enquiry to which no truthful answer can be given. The object of science is truth; therefore science alone, with all modesty be it said, can attain truth. Science will not ask the question — or, when it is merciful, abstains from asking the question — whether religion is true. So the reasonable and truthful man must, on that point, necessarily be agnostic: whether religion is true, he does not know.

This train of inferences follows — so far as it is permitted illogical inferences to follow at all — from the premise that the object of science is truth. Or, rather, it follows from that premise as we should now understand it, viz. that the object of historic science is historic truth. That is the object of the science of religion — to be true to the historic facts, to discover and to state them accurately. On the principle of the division of labour, or on the principle of taking one thing at a time, it is obviously wise that when we are endeavouring to discover the historic sequence of events, we should confine ourselves to that task and not suffer ourselves to be distracted and diverted by other and totally different considerations. The science of religion, therefore, is justified, in the opinion of all who are entitled to express an opinion, in steadfastly declining to consider any other point than the historic order of the facts with which it deals. But in so declining to go beyond its self-appointed task of reconstituting the historic order of events and tracing the evolution of religion, it does not, thereby, imply that it is impossible to place them, or correctly place them, in their order of value. To say that they have no value would be just as absurd as to say that works of literature or art have no literary or artistic value. To say that it is difficult to assign their value may be true, but is no argument against, it is rather a stimulus in favour of, making the attempt. And it is just the order value, the relative value, of forms of religion which is of absorbing interest to missionaries. ⌐It is a valuation which is essential to what I have already designated as the applied science of religion

Thus far in speaking of the distinction between the historic order in which the various forms of art, literature, and religion have occurred, and the order of value in which the soul of every man who is sensible either to art or to literature or to religion instinctively attempts to place them, I have necessarily assumed the position of one who looks backward over the past. It was impossible to compare and contrast the order value with the historic order, save by doing so. It was necessary to point out that the very same facts which can be arranged chronologically and in the order of their evolution can also be — and, as a matter of fact, by every man are — arranged more or less roughly, more or less correctly, or incorrectly, in the order of their value. It is now necessary for us to set our faces towards the future. I say "necessary" for the simple reason that the idea of "value" carries with it a reference to the future. If a thing has value, it is because we judge that it may produce some effect and serve some purpose which we foresee, or at least surmise. If, on looking back upon past history, we pronounce that an event had value, we do so because we see that it served, or might have served, some end of which we approve. Its value is relative in our eyes to some end or purpose which was relatively future to it. The objects which we aim at, the ends after which we strive, are in the future. Those things have value which may subserve our ends and help us to attain our purposes. And our purposes, our ends, and objects are in the future. There, there is hope and freedom, room to work, the chance of remedying the errors of the past, the opportunity to make some forward strides and to help others on.

It is the end we aim at, the object we strive for, the ideal we set before us, that gives value to what we do, and to what has been done by us and others. Now our ends, our objects, and our ideals are matters of the will, on which the will is set, and not merely matters of which we have intellectual apprehension. They are not past events but future possibilities. The conviction that we can attain them or attain toward them is not, when stated as a proposition, a proposition that can be proved, as a statement referring to the past may be proved: but it is a conviction which we hold, or a conviction which holds us, just as strongly as any conviction that we have about any past event of history. The whole action of mankind, every action that every man performs, is based upon that conviction. It is the basis of all that we do, of everything that is and has been done by us and others. And it is Faith. In that sign alone can the world be conquered.

When, then, the man of religion proposes by faith to conquer the world, he is simply doing, wittingly and in full consciousness of what he is doing, that which every man does in his every action, even though he may not know it. To make it a sneer or a reproach that religion is a mere matter of faith; to imagine that there is any better, or indeed that there is any other, ground of action, — is demonstrably unreasonable. The basis of such notions is, of course, the false idea that the man of sense acts upon knowledge, and that the man who acts on faith is not a sensible man. The error of such notions may be exposed in a sentence. What knowledge have we of the future? We have none. Absolutely none. We expect that nature will prove uniform, that causes will produce their effects. We believe the future will resemble, to some extent, the past. But we have no knowledge of the future; and such belief as we have about it, like all other belief,— whether it be belief in religion or in science,—is simply faith. When, then, the man of science consults the records of the past or the experiments of the present for guidance as to what will or may be, he is exhibiting his faith not in science, but in some reality, in some real being, in which is no shadow of turning. When the practical man uses the results of pure science for some practical end, he is taking them on faith and uses them in the further faith that the end he aims at can be realised, and shall by him be realised, if not in one way, then in another. The missionary, then, who uses the results of the science of religion, who seeks to benefit by an applied science of religion, is but following in the footsteps of the practical man, and using business methods toward the end he is going to realise.

The end he is going to realise is to convert men to Christianity. The faith in which he acts is that Christianity is the highest form which religion can take, the final form it shall take. As works of art or literature may be classed either according to order of history or order of value, so the works of the religious spirit may be classed, not only in chrono-logical order, but also in order of religious value. I am not aware that any proof can be given to show that any given period of art or literature is better than any other. The merits of Shakespeare or of Homer may be pointed out; and they may, or they may not, when pointed out, be felt. If they are felt, no proof is needed; if they are not, no proof is pos-sible. But they can be pointed out — by one who feels them. And they can be contrasted with the work of other poets in which they are less conspicu-ous. And the contrast may reveal the truth in a way in which otherwise it could never have been made plain.

I know no other way in which the relative values of different forms of religion can become known or be made known. You may have been tempted to reflect, whilst I have been speaking, that, on the principle I have laid down, there is no reason why there should not be five hundred applied sciences, or applications of the science, of religion, instead of one; for every one of the many forms of religion may claim to apply the science of religion to its own ends. To that I may reply first, that *a priori* you would expect that every nation would set up its own literature as the highest; but, as a matter of fact, you find Shakespeare generally placed highest amongst dramatists, Homer amongst epic poets. You do not find the conception of literary merit varying from nation to nation in such a way that there are as many standards of value as there are persons to apply them. You find that there tends to be one standard. Next, since the different forms of religion must be compared if their relative values are to be ascertained, the method of the applied science of religion must be the method of comparison. Whatever the outcome that is anticipated from the employment of the applied science, it is by the method of comparison that it must act. And one indication of genuine faith is readiness to employ that method, and assured confidence in the result of its employment. The missionary's life is the best, because the most concrete example of the practical working of the method of comparison; and the outcome of the comparison which is made by those amongst whom and for whom he works makes itself felt in their hearts, their lives, and sometimes in their conversion. It is the best example, because the value of a religion to be known must be felt. But though it is the best because it is the simplest, the most direct, and the most convincing, it is not that which addresses itself primarily to the reason, and it is not one which is produced by the applied science of religion. It is not one which can be produced by any science, pure or applied. The object of the applied science of religion is to enable the missionary himself to compare forms of religion, incidentally in order that he may know what by faith he feels, and without faith he could not feel, viz. that Christianity is the highest form; but still more in order that he may teach others, and may have at his command the facts afforded by the science of religion, wherewith to appeal, when necessary, to the reason and intelligence as well as to the hearts and feelings of those for whose salvation he is labouring.

The time has happily gone by when the mere idea of comparing Christianity with any other religion would have been rejected with horror as treasonous and treacherous.. The fact that that time has now gone by is in itself evidence of a stronger faith in Christianity. What, if it was not fear, at any rate presented the appearance of fear, has been banished; and we can and do, in the greater faith that has been vouchsafed to us, look with confidence on the proposal to compare Christianity with other religions. The truth cannot but gain thereby, and we rest on Him who is the way and the truth. We recognise fully and freely that comparison implies similarity, points of resemblance, ay! and even features of identity. And of that admission much has been made — and more than can be maintained. It has been pressed to mean that all forms of religion, from the lowest to the highest, are identical; that therefore there is nothing more or other in the highest than in the lowest; and that in the lowest you see how barbarous is religion and how unworthy of civilised man. Now, that course of argument is open to one obvious objection which would be fatal to it, even if it were the only objection, which it is not. That objection is that whether we are using the method of comparison for the purpose of estimating the relative values of different forms of religion; or whether we are using the comparative method of science, with the object of discovering and establishing facts, quite apart from the value they may have for any purpose they may be put to when they have been established; in either case, comparison is only applied, and can only be applied to things which, though they resemble one another, also differ from one another. It is because they differ, at first sight, that the discovery of their resemblance is important. And it is on that aspect of the truth that the comparative method of science dwells. Comparative philology, for instance, devotes itself to establishing resemblances between, say, the Indo-European languages, which for long were not suspected to bear any likeness to one another or to have any connection with each other. Those resemblances are examined more and more closely, are stated with more and more precision, until they are stated as laws of comparative philology, and recognised as laws of science to which there are no exceptions. Yet when the resemblances have been worked out to the furthest detail, no one imagines that Greek and Sanskrit are the same language, or that the differences between them are negligible. It is then surprising that any student of comparative religion should imagine that the discovery or the recognition of points of likeness between the religions compared will ever result in proving that the differences between them are negligible or non-existent. Such an inference is unscientific, and it has only to be stated to show that the student of comparative religion is but exercising a right common to all students of all sciences, when he claims that points of difference cannot be over-looked or thrust aside.

If, then, the student of the science of religion directs his attention primarily to the discovery of resemblances between religions which at first sight bear no more resemblance to one another than Greek did to the Celtic tongues; if the comparative method of science dwells upon the fact that things which differ from one another may also resemble one another, and that their resemblances may be stated in the form of scientific laws, — there is still another aspect of the truth, and it is that between things which resemble one another there are also differences. And the jury of the world will ultimately demand to know the truth and the whole truth.

Now, to get not only at the truth, but at the whole of the truth, is precisely the business of the applied science of religion, and is the very object of that which, in order to distinguish it from the comparative method of science, I have called the method of comparison. For the purposes of fair comparison not only must the resemblances, which the

comparative method of science dwells on, be
taken into account, but the differences, also, must be
weighed. And it is the business of the method of
comparison, the object of the applied science of
religion, to do both things. Neither of the two can
be dispensed with; neither is more important than
the other; but for the practical purposes of the
missionary it is important to begin with the resemblances; and on grounds of logic and of theory, the
resemblances must be first established, if the importance, nay! the decisive value, of the differences
is to go home to the hearts and minds of the missionary's hearers. The resemblances are there and
are to be studied ultimately in order to bring out
the differences and make them stand forth so plainly
as to make choice between the higher form of religion and the lower easy, simply because the difference is so manifest. Now, the missionary's hearer
could not know, much less appreciate, the difference,
the superiority of Christianity, as long as Christianity was unknown to him. And it is equally
manifest, though it has never been officially recognised until now and by the Hartford Theological
Seminary, that neither can the missionary ade-
quately set forth the superiority of Christianity to

the lower forms of religion, unless he knows something about them and about the points in which their inferiority consists. Hitherto he has had to learn that for himself, as he went on, and, as it were, by rule of thumb. But, on business principles, economy of labour and efficiency in work will be better secured if he is taught before he goes out, and is taught on scientific methods. What he has to learn is the resemblances between the various forms of religion, the differences between them, and the relative values of those differences.

It may perhaps be asked, Why should those differences exist? And if the question should be put, I am inclined to say that to give the answer is beyond the scope of the applied science of religion. The method of comparison assumes that the differences do exist, and it cannot begin to be employed unless and until they exist. They are and must be taken for granted, at any rate by the applied science of religion, and if the method of comparison is to be set to work. Indeed, if we may take the principle of evolution to be the differentiation of the homogeneous, we may go further and say that the whole theory of evolution, and not merely a particular historic science, such as the science of religion, postulates differentiation and the principle of difference, and does not explain it,— evolution cannot start, the homogeneous cannot be other than homogeneous, until the principle of difference and the power of differentiation is assumed.

That the science of religion at the end leaves untouched those differences between religions which it recognised at the beginning, is a point on which I insisted, as against those who unwarrantably proclaim the science to have demonstrated that all religions alike are barbarisms or survivals of barbarism. It is well, therefore, to bear that fact in mind when attempts are made to explain the existence of the differences by postulating a period when they were non-existent. That postulate may take form in the supposition that originally the true religion alone existed, and that the differences arose later. That is a supposition which has been made by more than one people, and in more ages than one. It carries with it the consequence that the history — it would be difficult to call it the evolution and impossible to call it the progress — of religion has been one of degradation generally. Owing, however, to the far-reaching and deep-penetrating influence of the theory of evolution, it has of late grown customary to assume that the movement, the course of religious history, has been in the opposite direction; and that it has moved upwards from the lowest forms of religion known to us, or from some form analogous to the lowest known forms, through the higher to the highest. This second theory, however different in its arrangement of the facts from the Golden Age theory first alluded to, is still fundamentally in agreement with it, inasmuch as it also assumes that the differences exhibited later in the history of religion at first were non-existent. Both theories assume the existence of the originally homogeneous, but they disagree as to the nature of the differences which supervened, and also as to the nature of the originally homogeneous.

I wish therefore to call attention to the simple truth that the facts at the disposal of the science of religion neither enable nor warrant us to decide between these two views. If we were to come to a decision on the point, we should have to travel far beyond the confines of the science of religion, or the widest bounds of the theory of evolution, and enquire why there should be error as well as truth — or, to put the matter very differently, why there should be truth at all. But if we started travelling

on that enquiry, we should not get back in time for
this course of lectures.   Fortunately it is not necessary to take a ticket for that journey — perhaps not
possible to secure a return ticket. We have only
to recognise that the science of religion confines
itself to constating and tracing the differences, and
does not attempt to explain why they should exist;
while the applied science of religion is concerned
with the practical business of bringing home the
difference between Christianity and other forms of
religion to the hearts of those whose salvation may
turn on whether the missionary has been properly
equipped for his task.

If, now, I announce that for the student of the
applied science it is advisable that he should turn
his attention in the first place to the lowest forms of
religion, the announcement need not be taken to
mean that a man cannot become a student of the
science of religion, whether pure or applied, unless
he assumes that the lowest is the most primitive
form.   The science of religion, as it pushes its
enquiries, may possibly come across — may even
already have come across — the lowest form to
which it is possible for man to descend.   But
whether that form is the most primitive as well as

the lowest, — still more, whether it is the most primitive because it is the lowest, — will be questions which will not admit of being settled offhand. And in the meantime we are not called upon to answer them in the affirmative as a *sine qua non* of being admitted students of the science.

The reason for beginning with the lowest forms is — as is proper in a practical science — a practical one. As I have already said, if the missionary is to succeed in his work, he must know and teach the difference and the value of the difference between Christianity and other religions. But difference implies similarity : we cannot specify the points of difference between two things without presupposing some similarity between them, — at any rate sufficient similarity to make a comparison of them profitable. Now, the similarity between the higher forms of religion is such that there is no need to demonstrate it, in order to justify our proceeding to dwell upon the differences. But the similarity between the higher and the lower forms is far from being thus obvious. Indeed, in some cases, for example in the case of some Australian tribes, there is alleged, by some students of the science of religion, to be such a total absence of similarity that we are entitled or compelled to recognise that however liberally, or loosely, we relax our definition of religion, we must pronounce those tribes to be without religion. The allegation thus made, the question thus raised, evidently is of practical importance for the practical purposes of the missionary. Where some resemblances exist between the higher and the lower forms of religion, those resemblances may be made, and should be made, the ground from which the missionary should proceed to point out by contrast the differences, and so to set forth the higher value of Christianity. But if no such resemblances should exist, they cannot be made a basis for the missionary's work. Without proceeding in this introductory lecture to discuss the question whether there are any tribes whatever that are without religion, I may point out that religion, in all its forms, is, in one of its aspects, a yearning and aspiration after God, a search after Him, peradventure we may find Him. And if it be alleged that in some cases there is no search after Him, — that amongst civilised men, amongst our own acquaintances, there is in some cases no search and no aspiration, and that therefore among the more backward peoples of the earth there may also be tribes to whom the very idea of

such a search is unknown, — then we must bear in
mind that a search, after any object whatever, may
be dropped, may even be totally abandoned; and
yet the heart may yearn after that which it is per-
suaded — or, it may be, is deluded into thinking —
it can never find. Perhaps, however, that way of
putting it may be objected to, on the ground that it
is a *petitio principii* and assumes the very fact it
is necessary to prove, viz. that the lowest tribes that
are or can be known to us have made the search
and given it up, whereas the contention is that they
have never made the search. That contention, I
will remark in passing, is one which never can be
proved. But to those who consider that it is probable in itself, and that it is a necessary stage in the
evolution of belief, I would point out that every
search is made in hope — or, it may be, in fear —
that search presupposes hope and fear. Vague, of
course, the hope may be; scarce conscious, if conscious at all, of what is hoped. But without hope,
until there are some dim stirrings, however vague,
search is unconceivable, and it is in and by the process of search that the hope becomes stronger and
the object sought more definite to view. Now,
inasmuch as it is doubtful whether any tribe of

people is without religion, it may reasonably be
held that the vast majority, at any rate, of the peoples
of the earth have proceeded from hope to aspiration
and to search; and if there should be found a tribe
which had not yet entered consciously on the search,
the reasonable conclusion would be not that it is
exempted from the laws which we see exemplified
in all other peoples, but that it is tending to obey
the same laws and is starting from the same point
as they, — that hope which is the desire of all nations and has been made manifest in the Son of
Man.

Whatever be the earliest history of that hope,
whatever was its nature and course in prehistoric
times, it has been worked out in history in many
directions, under the influence of many errors, into
many forms of religion. But in them all we feel
that there is the same striving, the same yearning;
and we see it with the same pity and distress as we
may observe the distorted motions of the man who,
though partially paralysed, yet strives to walk, and
move to the place where he would be. It is with
these attempts to walk, in the hope of giving help to
them who need it, that we who are here to-day are
concerned. We must study them, if we are to

understand them and to remedy them. And there is no understanding them, unless we recognise that in them all there is the striving and yearning after God, which may be cruelly distorted, but is always there.

It so happens that there has been great readiness on the part of students of the science of religion to recognise that belief in the continued existence of the soul after the death of the body has comparative universality amongst the lower races of mankind. Their yearning after continued existence developes into hope of a future life; and the hope, or fear, takes many forms: the continued existence may or may not be on this earth; it may or may not take the shape of a belief in the transmigration of souls; it sometimes does, and sometimes does not, lead to belief in the judgment of the dead and future punishments and rewards; it may or may not postulate the immortality of the soul; it may shrink to comparative, if not absolute, unimportance; or it may be dreaded and denounced by philosophy and even by religion. But whether dreaded or delighted in, whether developed by religion or denounced, the tendency to the belief is there — universal among mankind and ineradicable.

The parallel, then, between this belief and the belief or tendency to believe in God is close and instructive; and I shall devote my next lecture therefore to the belief in a future life among the primitive races of mankind. That belief manifests itself, as I shall hope to show, from the beginning, in a yearning hope for the continued existence of the beloved ones who have been taken from us by death, as well as in dread of the ghosts of those who during their life were feared. But in either case what it postulates and points to is man living in community with man. It implies society; and there again is parallel to religion. It is with the hopes and fears of the community as such that religion has to do: and it is from that point of view that I shall start when I come to deal with the subject of magic, and its resemblance to and difference from religion. Its resemblance is not accidental and the difference is not arbitrary: the difference is that between social and anti-social purposes. That difference, if borne in mind, may give us the clue to the real nature of fetishism, — a subject which will require a lecture to itself. I shall then proceed to a topic which has been ignored to a surprising extent by the science of religion; that is, the subject of prayer: and the light which is to be derived thence will, I trust, give fresh illumination to the meaning of sacrifice. The relation of religion to morality will then fall to be considered; and my final lecture will deal with the place of Christianity in the evolution of religion.

IMMORTALITY

THE missionary, like any other practical man, requires to know what science can teach him about the material on which he has to work. So far as is possible, he should know what materials are sound and can be used with safety in his constructive work, and what must be thrown aside, what must be destroyed, if his work is to escape dry-rot and to stand as a permanent edifice. He should be able to feel confidence, for instance, not merely that magic and fetichism are the negation of religion, but that in teaching that fact he has to support him the evidence collected by the science of religion; and he should have that evidence placed at his disposal for effective use, if need be.

It may be also that amongst much unsound material he will find some that is sound, that may be used, and that he cannot afford to cast away. He has to work upon our common humanity, upon the humanity common to him and his hearers. He has to remember that no man and no community of men ever is or has been or ever can be excluded from the search after God. And his duty, his chosen duty, is to help them in that search, and as far as may be to make the way clear for them, and to guide their feet in the right path. He will find that they have attempted to make paths for themselves; and it is not impossible that he will find that some of those paths for some distance do go in the right direction; that some of their beliefs have in them an element of truth, or a groping after truth which, rightly understood, may be made to lead to Christianity. It is with one of those beliefs — the belief in immortality — that I shall deal in this lecture.

It is a fact worthy of notice that the belief in immortality fills, I will not say a more important, but a more prominent, place in the hearts and hopes of uncivilised than of civilised man; and it is also a fact worthy of notice that among primitive men the belief in immortality is much less intimately bound up with religion than it comes to be at a later period of evolution. The two facts are probably not wholly without relation to one another. So long as the belief in immortality luxuriates and grows wild, so to speak, untrained and unrestrained by religion, it developes as the fancy wills, and lives by flattering the fancy. When, however, the relations of a future life to morality and religion come to be realised, when the conception of the next world comes to be moralised, then it becomes the subject of fear as well as of hope; and the fancy loses much of the freedom with which it tricked out the pictures that once it drew, purely according to its own sweet liking, of a future state. On the one hand, the guilty mind prefers not to dwell upon the day of reckoning, so long as it can stave off the idea; and it may succeed more or less in putting it on one side until the proximity of death makes the idea insistent. Thus the mind more or less deliberately dismisses the future life from attention. On the other hand, religion itself insists persistently on the fact that you have your duty here and now in this world to perform, and that the rest, the future consequences, you must leave to God. Thus, once more, and this time not from unworthy motives, attention is directed to this life rather than to the next; and it is this point that is critical for the fate both of the belief in immortality and of religion itself. At this point, religion may, as in the case of Buddhism it actually has done, formally give up and disavow belief in immortality. And in that case it sows the seed of its own destruction. Or it may recognise that the immortality of the soul is postulated by and essential to morality and religion alike. And in that case, even in that case alone, is religion in a position to provide a logical basis for morality and to place the natural desire for a future life on a firmer basis than the untutored fancy of primitive man could find for it.

It is then with primitive man or with the lower races that we will begin, and with "the comparative universality of their belief in the continued existence of the soul after the death of the body" (Tylor, *Primitive Culture*, II, 1). Now, the classical theory of this belief is that set forth by Professor Tylor in his *Primitive Culture*. Whence does primitive man get his idea that the soul continues to exist after the death of the body? the answer given is, in the first place, from the fact that man dreams. He dreams of distant scenes that he visits in his sleep; it is clear, from the evidence of those who saw his sleeping body, that his body certainly did not travel; therefore he or his soul must be separable from the body and must have travelled whilst his body lay unmoving and unmoved. But he also dreams of those who are now dead, and whose bodies he knows, it may be, to have been incinerated. The explanation then is obvious that they, too, or their souls, are separable from their bodies; and the fact that they survive death and the destruction of the body is demonstrated by their appearance in his dreams. About the reality of their appearance in his dreams he has no more doubt than he has about the reality of what he himself does and suffers in his dreams. If, however, the dead appeared only in his dreams, their existence after death might seem to be limited to the dream-time. But as a matter of fact they appear to him in his waking moments also: ghosts are at least as familiar to the savage as to the civilised man; and thus the evidence of his dreams, which first suggested his belief, is confirmed by the evidence of his senses.

Thus the belief in the continued existence of the soul after the death of the body is traced back to the action of dreams and waking hallucinations. Now, it is inevitable that the inference should be drawn that the belief in immortality has thus been tracked to its basis. And it is inevitable that those who start with an inclination to regard the belief as palpably absurd should welcome this exhibition of its evolution as proof conclusive that the belief could only have originated in and can only impose upon immature minds. To that doubtless it is a perfectly sound reply to say that the origin of a belief is one thing and its validity quite another. The way in which we came to hold the belief is a matter of historical investigation, and undoubtedly may form a very fascinating enquiry. But the question whether the belief is true is a question which has to be considered, no matter how I got it, just as the question whether I am committing a trespass or not in being on a piece of ground cannot be settled by any amount of explaining how I got there. Or, to put it in another way, the very risky path by which I have scrambled up a cliff does not make the top any the less safe when I have got there.

But though it is perfectly logical to insist on the distinction between the origin and the validity of any belief, and to refuse to question or doubt the validity of the belief in immortality merely because of the origin ascribed to it by authorities on primitive culture,—that is no reason why we should not examine the origin suggested for it, to see whether it is a satisfactory origin. And that is what I propose now to do. I wish to suggest first that belief in the appearance of the dead, whether to the dreamer or the ghost-seer, is an intellectual belief as to what occurs as a matter of fact; and next that thereby it is distinguished from the desire for immortality which manifests itself with comparative universality amongst the lower races.

Now, that the appearance of the dead, whether to the waking or the sleeping eye, is sufficient to start the intellectual belief will be admitted alike by those who do and those who do not hold that it is sufficient logically to warrant the belief. But to say that it starts the desire to see him or her whom we have lost, would be ridiculous. On the contrary, it would be much nearer the truth to say that it is the longing and the desire to see, once again, the loved one, that sets the mind a-dreaming, and first gives to the heart hope. The fact that, were there no desire for the continuance of life after the death of the body, the belief would never have caught on — that it either would never have arisen or would have soon ceased to exist — is shown by the simple consideration that only where the desire for the continuance of life after death dies down does the belief in immortality tend to wane. If any further evidence of that is required it may be found in the teaching of those

forms of philosophy and religion which endeavour
to dispense with the belief in immortality, for they
all recognise and indeed proclaim that they are based
on the denial of the desire and the will to live. If,
and only if — as, and only as — the desire to live,
here and hereafter, can be suppressed, can the belief in immortality be eradicated. The basis of the
belief is the desire for continued existence; and
that is why the attempt to trace the origin of the belief in immortality back to the belief in dreams and
apparitions is one which is not perfectly satisfactory;
it leaves out of account the desire without which the
belief would not be and is not operative.

But though it leaves out an element which is at
least as important as any element it includes, it
would be an error to take no account of what it does
contribute. It would be an error of this kind if we
closed our eyes to the fact that what first arrests
the attention of man, in the lower stages of his evolution, is the survival of others than himself. That
is the belief which first manifests itself in his heart
and mind; and what first reveals it to him is the appearance of the dead to his sleeping or his waking
eye. He does not first hope or believe that he himself will survive the death of the body and then go

on to infer that therefore others also will similarly survive. On the contrary, it is the appearance of others in his sleeping or waking moments that first gives him the idea; and it is only later and on reflection that it occurs to him that he also will have, or be, a ghost.

But though we must recognise the intellectual element in the belief and the intellectual processes which are involved in the belief, we must also take into account the emotional element, the element of desire. And first we should notice that the desire is not a selfish or self-regarding desire; it is the longing for one loved and lost, of the mother for her child, or of the child for its mother. It is desire of that kind which gives to dreams and apparitions their emotional value, without which they would have little significance and no spiritual importance. That is the direction in which we must look for the reason why, on the one hand, belief in the continuation of existence after death seems at first to have no connection with religion, while, on the other hand, the connection is ultimately shown by the evolution of belief to be so intimate that neither can attain its proper development without the other.

Dreams are occasions on which the longing for

one loved and lost manifests itself, but they are not the cause or the origin of the affection and the longing. But dreams are not exclusively, specially, or even usually the domain in which religion plays a part. Hence the visions of the night, in which the memory of the departed and the craving for reunion with them are manifested, bear no necessary reference to religion; and it is therefore possible, and *prima facie* plausible, to maintain that the belief in the immortality of the soul has its origin in a centre quite distinct from the sphere of religion, and that it is only very slowly, if at all, that the belief in immortality comes to be incorporated with religion. On the other hand, the very craving for reunion or continued communion with those who are felt not to be lost but gone before, is itself the feeling which is, not the base, but at the base, of religion. In the lowest forms to which religion can be reduced, or in which it manifests itself, religion is a bond of community; it manifests itself externally in joint acts of worship, internally in the feeling that the worshippers are bound together by it and united with the object of their worship. This feeling of communion is not a mere article of intellectual belief, nor is it imposed upon the members; it is what they themselves desire.

Höffding states the truth when he says that in its most rudimentary form we encounter "religion under the guise of desire"; but in saying so he omits the essence of the truth, that essence without which the truth that he partially enunciates may become wholly misleading,—he omits to say, and I think he fails to see, that the desire which alone can claim to be considered as religious is the desire of the community, not of the individual as such, and the desire of the community as united in common worship. The idea of religion as a bond of spiritual communion is implicit from the first, even though a long process of evolution be necessary to disentangle it and set it forth self-consciously. Now, it is precisely this spiritual communion of which man becomes conscious in his craving after reunion or continued communion with those who have departed this life. And it is with the history of his attempts to harmonise this desire with what he knows and demands of the universe otherwise, that we are here and now concerned.

So strong is that desire, so inconceivable is the idea that death ends all, and divorces from us forever those we have loved and lost awhile, that the lower races of mankind have been pretty generally driven to the conclusion that death is a mistake or due to a mistake. It is widely held that there is no such thing as a natural death. Men do of course die, they may be killed; but it is not an ordinance of nature that a man must be killed; and, if he is killed, his death is not natural. So strong is this feeling that when a man dies and his death is not obviously a case of murder, the inference which the savage prefers to draw is that the death is really a case of murder, but that the murder has been worked by witchcraft or magic. Amongst the Australian black fellows, as we are told by Messrs. Spencer and Gillen, "no such thing as natural death is realised by the native; a man who dies has of necessity been killed by some other man or perhaps even by a woman, and sooner or later that man or woman will be attacked;" consequently, "in very many cases there takes place what the white man, not seeing beneath the surface, not unnaturally describes as secret murder; but in reality . . . every case of such secret murder, when one or more men stealthily stalk their prey with the object of killing him, is in reality the exacting of a life for a life, the accused person being indicated by the so-called medicine man as one who has brought about the death of another man by magic, and whose life must therefore be forfeited" (*Native Tribes of Central Australia*, p. 48).

What underlies this idea that by man alone is death brought into the world is that death is unnatural and is no part of the original design of things. When the fact comes to be recognised undeniably that deaths not caused by human agency do take place, then the fact requires explanation; and the explanation on which primitive races, quite independently of each other, hit is that as death was no part of the original design of things, its introduction was due to accident or mistake. Either men were originally exempt from death, or they were intended to be exempt. If they were intended to be exempt, then the inference drawn is that the intention was frustrated by the carelessness of the agent intrusted with the duty of making men deathless. If they were originally exempt from death, then the loss of the exemption has to be accounted for. And in either case the explanation takes the form of a narrative which relates how the mistake took place or what event it was that caused the loss of the exemption. I need not quote examples of either class of narrative. What I wish to do is to emphasise the fact that by primitive man death is felt to be inconsistent with the scheme of things. First, therefore, he denies that it can come in the course of nature, though he admits that it may be procured by the wicked man in the way of murder or magic. And it is at this stage that his hope of reunion with those loved and lost scarcely stretches beyond the prospect of their return to this world. Evidence of this stage is found partly in tales such as those told of the mother who returns to revisit her child, or of persons restored to life. Stories of this latter kind come from Tasmania, Australia, and Samoa, amongst other places, and are found amongst the Eskimo and American Indians, as well as amongst the Fjorts (J. A. MacCullough, *The Childhood of Fiction*, ch. IV). Even more direct evidence of the emotion which prompts these stories is afforded by the Ho dirge, quoted by Professor Tylor (*P. C.*, II, 32, 33) : —

> "We never scolded you; never wronged you;
> Come to us back !
> We ever loved and cherished you; and have lived long together
> Under the same roof;
> Desert it not now !
> The rainy nights and the cold blowing days are coming on;
> Do not wander here !
> Do not stand by the burnt ashes; come to us again !
> You cannot find shelter under the peepul, when the rain comes
> down,

The saul will not shield you from the cold bitter wind.
> Come to your home!
It is swept for you and clean; and we are there who loved you
ever;
And there is rice put for you and water;
> Come home, come home, come to us again!"

In these verses it is evident that the death of the body is recognised as a fact. It is even more manifest that the death of the body is put aside as weighing for naught against the absolute conviction that the loved one still exists. But reunion is sought in this world; another world is not yet thought of. The next world has not yet been called into existence to redress the sorrows and the sufferings of this life. Where the discovery of that solution has not been made, the human mind seeks such consolation as may be found elsewhere. If the aspiration, "come to us, come to us again," can find no other realisation, it welcomes the reappearance of the lost one in another form. In Australia, amongst the Euahlayi tribe, the mother who has lost her baby or her young child may yet believe that it is restored to her and born again in the form of another child. In West Africa, according to Miss Kingsley, "the new babies as they arrived in the family were shown a selection of small articles belonging to deceased members whose souls

were still absent, — the thing the child caught hold
of identified him. 'Why, he's Uncle John; see!
he knows his own pipe;' or 'That's Cousin Emma;
see! she knows her market calabash;' and so on."
But it is not only amongst Australian black fellows
or West African negroes that the attempt is made
to extract consolation for death from the speculation
that we die only to be reborn in this world. The
theory of rebirth is put forward by a distinguished
student of Hegel — Dr. McTaggart — in a work
entitled *Some Dogmas of Religion*. It is admitted
by Dr. McTaggart to be true that we have no memory
whatever of our previous stages of existence; but he
declares, "we may say that, in spite of the loss of
memory, it is the same person who lives in the suc-
cessive lives" (p. 130); and he appears to find the
same consolation as his remote forefathers did in
looking forward to a future stage of existence in
which he will have no more memory of his present
existence, and no more reason to believe in it, than
he now has memory of, or reason to believe in, his
preëxistence. "It is certain," he says, "that in
this life we remember no previous lives," and he
accepts the position that it is equally certain we shall
have in our next life absolutely no memory of our

present existence. That, of course, distinguishes
Dr. McTaggart from the West African Uncle John
who, when he is reborn, at any rate "knows his own
pipe."

The human mind, as I have said, seeks such consolation as it may find in the doctrine of rebirth.
It finds evidence of rebirth either in the behaviour
of the new-born child or in its resemblance to deceased relations. But it also comes to the conclusion that the reincarnation may be in animal form.
Whether that conclusion is suggested by the strangely
human expression in the eyes of some animals, or
whether it is based upon the belief in the power of
transformation, need not be discussed. It is beyond doubt that transformation is believed in: the
Cherokee Indian sings a verse to the effect that he becomes a real wolf; and "after stating that he has
become a real wolf, the songster utters a prolonged
howl, and paws the ground like a wolf with his feet"
(Frazer, *Kingship*, p. 71). Indeed, identity may be
attained or manifested without any process of transformation; in Australia, amongst the Dieri tribe,
the head man of a totem consisting of a particular
sort of a seed is spoken of by his people as being the
plant itself which yields the seed (*ib.*, p. 109).

Where such beliefs are prevalent, the doctrine of the reincarnation of the soul in animal form will obviously arise at the stage of evolution which we are now discussing, that is to say when the soul is not yet supposed to depart to another world, and must therefore manifest itself in this world in one way or another, if not in human shape, then in animal form. In the form of what animal the deceased will be reincarnated is a question which will be answered in different ways. Purely fortuitous circumstances may lead to particular animals being considered to be the reincarnation of the deceased. Or the fact that the deceased has a particular animal for totem may lead the survivors to expect his reappearance in the form of that particular animal. The one fact of importance for our present purpose is that at its origin the belief in animal reincarnation had no necessary connection with the theory of future punishments and rewards. At the stage of evolution in which the belief in transmigration arose many animals were the object of genuine respect because of the virtues of courage, etc., which were manifested by them; or because of the position they occupied as totems. Consequently no loss of status was involved when the soul transmigrated from a human to an animal form. No notion of punishment was involved in the belief.

The doctrines of reincarnation and transmigration belong to a stage in the evolution of belief, or to a system of thought, in which the conviction that the death of the body does not entail the destruction of the soul is undoubted, but from which the conception, indeed the very idea, of another world than this is excluded. That conception begins to manifest itself where ancestor worship establishes itself; but the manifestation is incomplete. Deceased chieftains and heroes, who have been benefactors to the tribe, are remembered; and the good they did is remembered also. They are themselves remembered as the doers of good; and their spirits are naturally conceived as continuing to be benevolent, or ready to confer benefits when properly approached. But thus envisaged, they are seen rather in their relation to the living than in their relation to each other. It is their assistance in this world that is sought; their condition in the next world is of less practical importance and therefore provokes less of speculation, in the first instance. But when speculation is provoked, it proves ultimately fatal to ancestor worship.

First, it may lead to the question of the relation of the spirits of the deceased benefactors to the god or gods of the community. There will be a tendency to blur the distinction between the god and his worshippers, if any of the worshippers come to be regarded as being after death spirits from whom aid may be invoked and to whom offerings must be made. And if the distinction ceases after death, it is difficult and sometimes impossible to maintain it during life; an emperor who is to be deified after death may find his deification beginning before his death. Belief in such deification may be accepted by some members of the community. Others will regard it as proof that religion is naught; and yet others will be driven to seek for a form of religion which affords no place for such deifications, but maintains explicitly that distinction between a god and his worshippers which is present in the most rudimentary forms of religion.

But though the tendency of ancestor worship is to run this course and to pass in this way out of the evolution of religion, it may be arrested at the very outset, if the religious spirit is, as it has been in one case at least, strong enough to stand against it at the beginning. Thus, amongst the Jews there was a tendency to ancestor worship, as is shown by the fact of its prohibition. But it was stamped out; and it was stamped out so effectually that belief in the continued existence of the soul after death ceased for long to have any practical influence, "Generally speaking, the Hebrews regarded the grave as the final end of all sentient and intelligent existence, 'the land where all things are forgotten'" (Smith's *Dictionary of the Bible*, s.v. Sheol). "In death," the Psalmist says to the Lord, "there is no remembrance of thee: in Sheol who shall give thee thanks?" "Shall they that are deceased arise and praise thee? Shall thy loving-kindness be declared in the grave?" or "thy righteousness in the land of forgetfulness?" Thus the Sheol of the Old Testament remains to testify to the view taken of the state of the dead by a people amongst whom the worship of ancestors was arrested at the outset. Amongst such a people the dead are supposed simply to continue in the next world as they left this: "in Sheol the kings of the nations have their thrones, and the mighty their weapons of war," just as in Virgil the ghost of Deiphobus still shows the ghastly wounds by which he perished (Jevons, *History of Religion*, p. 301).

This continuation theory, the view that the dead continue in the next world as they left this, means that, to the people who entertain it, the dead are merely a memory. It is forbidden to think of them as doing anything, as affecting the living in any way. They are conceived as powerless to gratify the wishes of the living, or to thwart them. Where the Lord God is a jealous God, religion cannot tolerate the idea that any other spirit should be conceived as usurping His functions, still less that such spirits should receive the offerings and the prayers which are the due of Him alone. But though the dead are thus reduced to a mere memory, the memory itself does not and cannot die. Accordingly the dead, or rather those whose bodies are dead, continue to live. But, as they exercise no action in, or control over, the world of the living, their place of abode comes to be regarded as another world, to which they are confined. Speculation, therefore, where speculation is made, as to the case of the inhabitants of this other world, must take the direction of enquiring as to their fate. Where speculation is not made, the dead are conceived merely to continue to be as they are remembered to have been in this life. But, if there is to be room for any speculation

at all, there must be assumed to be some diversity
in their fate, and therefore some reason, intelligible
to man, for that diversity. That is a conclusion to
which tribes attain who have apparently gone through
no period of ancestor worship, — indeed, ancestor
worship only impedes or defers the attainment of
that conclusion. The diversity of fate could only
consist in the difference between being where you
would be and being where you would not. But
the reasons for that diversity may be very different
amongst different peoples. First, where religion
is at its lowest or is in its least developed form, the
gods are not the cause of the diversity nor do they
seem concerned in it. Such diversity as there is
seems in its simplest form merely to be a continuance
of the social distinctions which prevail among the
living: the high chieftains rest in a calm, plenteous,
sunny land in the sky; while "all Indians of low
degree go deep down under the earth to the land of
Chay-her, with its poor houses and no salmon and
no deer, and blankets so small and thin, that when
the dead are buried the friends often bury blankets
with them" (Tylor, *P. C.*, II, 85). Elsewhere, it
is not social distinctions, but moral, that make the
difference: "the rude Tupinambas of Brazil think

the souls of such as had lived virtuously, that is to say who have well avenged themselves and eaten many of their enemies," (*ib.*) rejoin the souls of their fathers in the happy land, while the cowards go to the other place. Thus, though the distinctions in the next world do not seem originally to have sprung from or to have been connected with morality, and still less with religion, they are, or may be at a very early period, seized upon by the moral consciousness as containing truth or implying it, when rightly understood. Truth indeed of the highest import for morality is implied in the distinctions thus essayed to be drawn. But before the truth implicit could be made explicit, it was necessary that the distinctions should be recognised to have their basis in religion. And that was impossible where religion was at its lowest or in its least developed form.

From the fact that on the one hand the conception of a future life in another world, when it arose amongst people in a low stage of religious development, bore but little moral and no religious fruit; and on the other, where it did yield fruit, there had been a previous period when religion closed its eyes as far as possible to the condition of the dead

in Hades or in Sheol, — we may draw the inference
that the conception of the future state formed by such
people, as "the rude Tupinambas of Brazil" had
to be sterilised, so to speak, — to be purified from
associations dangerous both to morality and religion. We may fairly say that as a matter of fact
that was the consequence which actually happened,
and that both in Greece and Judæa the prospect of a
future life at one time became practically a *tabula
rasa* on which might be written a fairer message of
hope than had ever been given before.   In Greece
the message was written, indeed, and was received
with hope by the thousands who joined in the cele-
bration of the mysteries.   But the characters in
which it was written faded soon.   The message
was found to reveal nothing.   It revealed nothing
because it demanded nothing.   It demanded neither
a higher life nor a higher conception of the deity.
It did not set forth a new and nobler morality; and
it accommodated itself to the existing polytheism.
What it did do was to familiarise the Hellenic world
with the conviction that there was a life hereafter,
better than this life; and that the condition of its
attainment was communion with the true God,
peradventure He could be found.   It was by this

conviction and this expectation that the ground was prepared, wherever Hellenism existed, for the message that was to come from Israel.

From the beginning, or let us say in the lowest forms in which religion manifests itself, religion is the bond in which the worshippers are united with one another and with their God. The community which is thus united is at first the earliest form of society, whatever that form may have been, in which men dwell together for their common purposes. It is the fact that its members have common purposes and common interests which constitute them a community; and amongst the common interests without which there could be no community is that of common worship: knowledge of the *sacra*, being confined to the members of the community, is the test by which members are known, outsiders excluded, and the existence of the community as a community secured. At this stage, in a large number of societies — negro, Malayo-Polynesian, North American Indians, Eskimo, Australians — the belief in reincarnation takes a form in which the presence of souls of the departed is recognised as necessary to the very conception of the community. Thus in Alaska, among the Unalits of St. Michael's

Bay, a festival of the dead is observed, the equivalent of which appears to be found amongst all the Eskimo. M. Mauss (*L'Année Sociologique*, IX, 99) thus describes it: "It comprises two essential parts. It begins with praying the souls of the dead graciously to consent to reincarnate themselves for the moment in the namesake which each deceased person has; for the custom is that in each station the child last born always takes the name of the last person who has died. Then these living representatives of the deceased receive presents, and having received them the souls are dismissed from the abodes of the living to return to the land of the dead. Thus at this festival not only does the group regain its unity, but the rite reconstitutes the ideal group which consists of all the generations which have succeeded one another from the earliest times. Mythical and historic ancestors as well as later ones thus mingle with the living, and communion between them is conducted by means of the exchange of presents." Amongst people other than the Eskimo, a new-born child not only takes the name of the last member of the family or clan who has died, but is regarded as the reincarnation of the deceased. "Thus the number of individuals, of names, of souls, of social functions in the clan is limited; and the life of the clan consists in the death and rebirth of individuals who are always identically the same" (*l.c.* 267).

The line of evolution thus followed by the belief in reincarnation results in the total separation of the belief from morality and from religion, and results in rendering it infertile alike for morality, religion, and progress in civilisation generally. Where the belief in reincarnation takes the form of belief in the transmigration of the soul into some animal form, it may be utilised for moral purposes, provided that the people amongst whom the belief obtains have otherwise advanced so far as to see that the punishments and rewards which are essential to the development of morality are by no means always realised in this life. When that conviction has established itself, the reincarnation theory will provide machinery by which the belief in future punishments and rewards can be conceived as operative: rebirth in animal form, if the belief in it already exists, may be held out as a deterrent to wrongdoing. That is, as a matter of fact, the use to which the belief has been put by Buddhism. The form and station in which the deceased will be re-

born is no longer, as amongst the peoples just mentioned, conceived to be determined automatically,
so to speak, but is supposed to depend on the moral
qualities exhibited during life. If this view of the
future life has struck deeper root and has spread
over a greater surface than the doctrine taught in
the Greek mysteries ever did, the reason may probably be found in the fact that the Greek mysteries
had no higher morality to teach than was already
recognised, whilst the moral teaching of the Buddha
was far more exalted and far more profoundly true
than anything that had been preached in India
before. If a moral system by itself, on its own
merits, were capable of affording a sure foundation
for religion, Buddhism would be built upon a rock.
To the spiritual community by which man may be
united to his fellow-man and to his God, morality
is essential and indispensable. But the moral life
derives its value solely from the fact that on it
depends, and by means of it is realised, that communion of man with God after which man has from
the beginning striven. If then that communion and
the very possibility of that communion is denied,
the denial must prove fatal alike to religion and to
morality. Now, that is the denial which Buddhism

makes. But the fact of the denial is obscured to
those who believe, and to those who would like to
believe, in Buddhism, by the way in which it is made.
It is made in such a way that it appears and is
believed to be an affirmation instead of a denial.
Communion with God is declared to be the final end
to which the transmigration of souls conducts. But
the communion to which it leads is so intimate that
the human soul, the individual, ceases to be. Obviously, therefore, if it ceases to be, the communion
also must cease; there is no real communion sub-
sisting between two spirits, the human and the divine,
for two spirits do not exist, but only one. If this
way of stating the case be looked upon with suspicion as possibly not doing justice to the teaching
of Buddhism, or as pressing unduly far the union
between the human and the divine which is the
ultimate goal of the transmigration of souls, the
reply is that in truth the case against Buddhism
is stronger than appears from this mode of stating
it. To say that from the Buddhist point of view
the human soul, the individual, eventually ceases to
be, is indeed an incorrect way of putting the matter.
It implies that the human soul, the individual, now
is; and hereafter ceases to be. But so far from

admitting that the individual now is, the Buddhist doctrine is that the existence of the soul, now, is mere illusion, *mâyâ*. It is therefore logical enough, and at any rate self-consistent, to say that hereafter, when the series of transmigrations is complete, the individual will not indeed cease to be, for he never was, but the illusion that he existed will be dissipated. Logically again, it follows from this that if the existence of the individual soul is an illusion from the beginning, then there can strictly speaking be no transmigration of souls, for there is no soul to transmigrate. But with perfect self-consistency Buddhism accepts this position: what is transmitted from one being to the next in the chain of existences is not the individuality or the soul, but the character. Professor Rhys Davids says (*Hibbert Lectures*, pp. 91, 92): "I have no hesitation in maintaining that Gotama did not teach the transmigration of souls. What he did teach would be better summarized, if we wish to retain the word transmigration, as the transmigration of character. But it would be more accurate to drop the word transmigration altogether when speaking of Buddhism, and to call its doctrine the doctrine of karma. Gotama held that after the death of any being,

whether human or not, there survived nothing at
all but that being's 'karma,' the result, that is, of
its mental and bodily actions." "He discarded the
theory of the presence, within each human body,
of a soul which could have a separate and eternal
existence. He therefore established a new identity
between the individuals in the chain of existence,
which he, like his forerunners, acknowledged, by
the new assertion that that which made two beings
to be the same being was — not soul, but — karma"
(ib., pp. 93, 94). Thus once more it appears that
there can be no eventual communion between
the human soul, at the end of its chain of existence,
and the divine, for the reason, not that the human
soul ultimately ceases to be, but that it never is or
was, and therefore neither transmigrates from one
body to another, nor is eventually absorbed in the
âtmân.

Logically consistent though this train of argument be, it leaves unanswered the simple question,
How can the result of my actions have any interest
for me — not hereafter, but at the present moment —
if I not only shall not exist hereafter but do not exist
at the present moment? It is not impossible for a
man who believes that his existence will absolutely

cease at death to take some interest in and labour for the good of others who will come after him; but it is impossible for a man who does not exist now to believe in anything whatever. And it is on that fundamental absurdity that Buddhism is built: it is directed to the conversion of those who do not exist to be converted, and it is directed to the object of relieving from existence those who have no existence from which to be relieved.

Where then lies the strength of Buddhism, if as a logical structure it is rent from top to bottom by glaring inconsistency? It lies in its appeal to the spirit of self-sacrifice. What it denounces, from beginning to end, is the will to live. The reason why it denounces the will to live is that that will manifests itself exclusively in the desires of the individual; and it is to the desires of man that all the misery in the world are directly due. Destroy those desires by annihilating the will to live — and in no other way can they be destroyed — and the misery of the world will cease. The only termination to the misery of the world which Buddhism can imagine is the voluntary cessation of life which will ultimately ensue on the cessation of the will to live. And the means by which that is to be brought about is the uprooting and destruction of the self-regarding desires by means of the higher morality of self-sacrifice. What the Buddhist overlooks is that the uprooting and destruction of the self-regarding desires results, not in the annihilation, but in the purification and enhanced vitality, of the self. that uproots them. The outcome of the unselfish and self-sacrificing life is not the destruction of individuality, but its highest realisation. Now, it is only in society and by living for others that this unselfishness and self-sacrifice can be carried out; man can only exist and unselfishness can only operate in society, and society means the communion of man with his fellows. It is true that only in society can selfishness exist; but it is recognized from the beginning as that which is destructive of society, and it is therefore condemned alike by the morality and the religion of the society. The communion of man with his fellows and his God is hindered, impeded, and blocked wholly and solely by his self-regarding desires; it is furthered and realised solely by his unselfish desires. But his unselfish desires involve and imply his existence — I was going to say, just as much, I mean — far more than his selfish desires, for they imply, and are only possible on, the assumption of

the existence of his fellow-man, and of his communion with him. Nay! more, by the testimony
of Buddhism itself as well as of the religious experience of mankind at large, the unselfish desires,
the spirit of self-sacrifice, require both for their
logical and their emotional justification, still more
for their practical operation, the faith that by means
of them the will of God is carried out, and that in
them man shows likest God. It is in them and by
them that the communion of man with his fellow-
man and with his God is realised. It is the faith
that such communion, though it may be interrupted,
can never be entirely broken which manifests itself
in the belief in immortality. That belief may take
shape in the idea that the souls of the departed
revisit this earth temporarily in ghostly form, or
more permanently as reincarnated in the new-born
members of the tribe; it may body forth another
world of bliss or woe, and if it is to subserve the
purposes of morality, it must so do; nay! more, if
it is to subserve the purposes of morality, it is into
the presence of the Lord that the soul must go. But
in any and whatever shape the belief takes, the soul
is conceived or implied to be in communion with
other spirits. There is no other way in which it is

possible to conceive the existence of a soul; just as any particle of matter, to be comprehended in its full reality, implies not only every other particle of matter but the universe which comprehends them, so the existence of any spirit logically implies not only the existence of every other but also of Him without whom no one of them could be.

It is in this belief in the communion of spirits wherever he may find it — and where will he not? — that the missionary may obtain a leverage for his work. It is a sure basis for his operations because the desire for communion is universal; and Christianity alone, of the religions of the world, teaches that self-sacrifice is the way to life eternal.

MAGIC

OF all the topics which present themselves to the student of the science of religion for investigation and explanation there is none which has caused more diversity of opinion, none which has produced more confusion of thought, than magic. The fact is that the belief in magic is condemned alike by science and religion, — by the one as essentially irrational, and by the other as essentially irreligious. But though it is thus condemned, it flourishes, where it does flourish, as being science, though of a more secret kind than that usually recognised, or as being a more potent application of the rites and ceremonies of religion. It is indeed neither science nor religion; it lives by mimicking one or other or both. In the natural history of belief it owes its survival, so long as it does survive, to its "protective colouring" and its power of mimicry. It is, always and everywhere, an error, — whether tried by the canons of science or religion;

but it lives, as error can only live, by posing and passing itself off as truth.

If now the only persons deceived by it were the persons who believed in it, students of the science of religion would have been saved from much fruitless controversy. But so subtly protective is its colouring that some scientific enquirers have confidently and unhesitatingly identified it with religion, and have declared that magic is religion, and religion is magic. The tyranny of that error, however, is now well-nigh overpast. It is erroneous, and we may suppose is seen to be erroneous, in exactly the same way as it would be to say that science is magic, and magic science. The truth is that magic in one aspect is a colourable imitation of science: "in short," as Dr. Frazer says (*Early History of the Kingship*, p. 38), "magic is a spurious system of natural law." That is, we must note, it is a system which is spurious in our eyes, but which, to those who believed in it, was "a statement of the rules which determine the sequence of events throughout the world — a set of precepts which human beings observe in order to compare their ends" (*ib.*, p. 39).

The point, then, from which I wish to start is that

magic, as it is now viewed by students of the science of religion, on the one hand is a spurious system of natural law or science, and on the other a spurious system of religion.

Our next point is that magic could not be spurious for those who believed in it : they held that they knew some things and could do things which ordinary people did not know and could not do; and, whether their knowledge was of the secrets of nature or of the spirit world, it was not in their eyes spurious.

Our third point is more difficult to explain, though it will appear not merely obvious, but self-evident, if I succeed in explaining it. It will facilitate the work of explanation, if you will for the moment suppose — without considering whether the supposition is true or not — that there was a time when no one had heard that there was such a thing as magic. Let us further suppose that at that time man had observed such facts as that heat produces warmth, that the young of animals and man resemble their parents : in a word, that he had attained more or less consciously to the idea, as a matter of observation, that like produces like, and as a matter of practice that like may be produced by like. Having attained to that practical idea, he will of course work it not only for all that it is worth, but for more. That is indeed the only way he has of finding out how much it is good for; and it is only repeated failure which will convince him that here at length he has reached the limit, that in this particular point things do not realise his expectations, that in this instance his anticipation of nature has been "too previous." Until that fact has been hammered into him, he will go on expecting and believing that in this instance also like will produce like, when he sets it to work; and he will be perfectly convinced that he is employing the natural and reasonable means for attaining his end. As a matter of fact, however, as we with our superior knowledge can see, in the first place those means never can produce the desired effect; and next, the idea that they can, as it withers and before it finally falls to the ground, will change its colour and assume the hue of magic. Thus the idea that by whistling you can produce a wind is at first as natural and as purely rational as the idea that you can produce warmth by means of fire. There is nothing magical in either. Both are matter-of-fact applications of the practical maxim that like produces like.

That, then, is the point which I have been wishing
to make, the third of the three points from which
I wish to start. There are three ways of looking
at identically the same thing, *e.g.* whistling to produce a wind. First, we may regard it, and I suggest
that it was in the beginning regarded, as an application, having nothing to distinguish it from
any other application, of the general maxim that
like produces like. The idea that eating the flesh
of deer makes a man timid, or that if you wish to
be strong and bold you should eat tiger, is, in this
stage of thought, no more magical than is the idea
of drinking water because you are dry.

Next, the idea of whistling to produce a wind,
or of sticking splinters of bone into a man's foot-
prints in order to injure his feet, may be an idea
not generally known, a thing not commonly done,
a proceeding not generally approved of. It is thus
marked off from the commonplace actions of
drinking water to moisten your parched throat or
sitting by a fire to get warm. When it is thus
marked off, it is regarded as magic: not every one
knows how to do it, or not every one has the power
to do it, or not every one cares to do it. That is
the second stage, the heyday of magic.

The third and final stage is that in which no educated person believes in it, when, if a man thinks to get a wind by whistling he may whistle for it. These three ways of looking at identically the same thing may and do coexist. The idea of whistling for a wind is for you and me simply a mistaken idea; but possibly at this moment there are sailors acting upon the idea and to some of them it appears a perfectly natural thing to do, while to others there is a flavour of the magical about it. But though the three ways may and do coexist, it is obvious that our way of looking at it is and must be the the latest of the three, for the simple reason that an error must exist before it can be exploded. I say that our way of looking at it must be the latest, but in saying so I do not mean to imply that this way of looking at it originates only at a late stage in the history of mankind. On the contrary, it is present in a rudimentary form from very early times; and the proof is the fact generally recognised that magicians amongst the lowest races, though they may believe to a certain extent in their own magical powers, do practise a good deal of magic which they themselves know to be fraudulent. Progress takes place when other people also, and a steadily increasing number of people, come to see that it is fraudulent.

In the next place, just as amongst very primitive peoples we see that some magic is known by some people, viz. the magicians themselves, to be fraudulent, though other people believe in it; so, amongst very primitive peoples, we find beliefs and practices existing which have not yet come to be regarded as magical, though they are such as might come, and do elsewhere come, to be considered pure magic. Thus, for instance, when Cherokee Indians who suffer from rheumatism abstain from eating the flesh of the common grey squirrel "because the squirrel eats in a cramped position, which would clearly aggravate the pangs of the rheumatic patient" (Frazer, *History of the Kingship*, p. 70), or when "they will not wear the feathers of the bald-headed buzzard for fear of themselves becoming bald" (*ib.*), they are simply following the best medical advice of their day, — they certainly do not imagine they are practising magic, any more than you or I do when we are following the prescriptions of our medical adviser. On the contrary, it is quite as obvious, then, that the feathers of the bald-headed buzzard are infectious as it is now that the clothes of a fever patient are infectious. Neither proposition, to be accepted as true, requires us to believe in magic: either might spring up where magic had never been heard of. And, if that is the case, it simply complicates things unnecessarily to talk of magic in such cases. The tendency to believe that like produces like is not a consequence of or a deduction from a belief in magic: on the contrary, magic has its root or one of its roots in that tendency of the human mind. But though that tendency helps to produce magic amongst other things, magic is not the only thing which it produces: it produces beliefs such as those of the Cherokees just quoted, which are no more magical than the belief that fire produces warmth, or that *causa aequat effectum*, that an effect is, when analysed, indistinguishable from the conditions which constitute it.

To attempt to define magic is a risky thing; and, instead of doing so at once, I will try to mark off proceedings which are not magical; and I would venture to say that things which it is believed any one can do, and felt that any one may do, are not magical in the eyes of those who have that belief and that feeling. You may abstain from eating squirrel or wearing fine feathers because of the consequences; and every one will think you are showing your common sense. You may hang up the bones of animals you have killed, in order to attract more animals of the like kind; and you are simply practising a dodge which you think will be useful. Wives whose husbands are absent on hunting or fighting expeditions may do or abstain from doing things which, on the principle that like produces like, will affect their husbands' success; and this application of the principle may be as irrational — and as perfectly natural — as the behaviour of the beginner at billiards whose body writhes, when he has made his stroke, in excess of sympathy with the ball which just won't make the cannon. In both cases the principle acted on, — deliberately in the one case, less voluntarily in the other, — the instinctive feeling is that like produces like, not as a matter of magic but as a matter of fact. If the behaviour of the billiard player is due to an impulse which is in itself natural and in his case is not magical, we may fairly take the same view of the hunter's wife who abstains from spinning for fear the game should turn and wind like the spindle and the hunter be unable to hit it (Frazer,

p. 55). The principle in both cases is that like
produces like. Some applications of that principle
are correct; some are not. The incorrectness of
the latter is not at once discovered: the belief in
their case is erroneous, but is not known to be erroneous. And unless we are prepared to take up the
position that magic is the only form of erroneous
belief which is to be found amongst primitive men,
we must endeavour to draw a line between those
erroneous beliefs which are magical and those
erroneous beliefs which are not. The line will
not be a hard and fast line, because a belief which
originally had nothing magical about it may come
to be regarded as magical. Indeed, on the assumption that belief in magic is an error, we have to
enquire how men come to fall into the error. If
there is no such thing as magic, how did man come
to believe that there was? My suggestion is that
the rise of the belief is not due to the introduction
of a novel practice, but to a new way of looking at
an existing practice. It is due in the first instance
to the fact that the practice is regarded with disapproval as far as its consequences are concerned
and without regard to the means employed to produce them. Injury to a member of the community,

especially injury which causes death, is viewed
by the community with indignant disapproval.
Whether the death is produced by actual blows or
"by drawing the figure of a person and then stabbing
it or doing it any other injury" (Frazer, p. 41),
it is visited with the condemnation of the community. And consequently all such attempts "to
injure or destroy an enemy by injuring or destroy-
ing an effigy of him" (*ib.*), whenever they are made,
whether they come off or not, are resented and
disapproved by society. On the other hand,
sympathetic or homœopathic magic of this kind,
when used by the hunter or the fisherman to secure
food, meets with no condemnation. Both assassin
and hunter use substantially the same means to
effect their object; but the disapproval with which
the community views the object of the assassin is
extended also to the means which he employs.
In fine, the practice of using like to produce like
comes to be looked on with loathing and with dread
when it is employed for antisocial purposes. Any
one can injure or destroy his private enemy by
injuring an effigy of him, just as any one can injure
or destroy his enemy by assaulting and wounding
him. But though any one may do this, it is felt

that no one ought to do it. Such practices are
condemned by public opinion. Further, as they
are condemned by the community, they are *ipso
facto* offensive to the god of the community. To
him only those prayers can be offered, and by him
only those practices can be approved, which are
not injurious to the community or are not felt by
the community to be injurious. That is the reason
why such practices are condemned by the religious
as well as by the moral feeling of the community.
And they are condemned by religion and morality
long before their futility is exposed by science or
recognised by common sense. When they are
felt to be futile, there is no call upon religion or
morality especially to condemn the practices —
though the intention and the will to injure our
fellow-man remains offensive both to morality
and religion. With the means adopted for realising
the will and carrying out the intention, morality
and religion have no concern. If the same or
similar means can be used for purposes consistent
with the common weal, they do not, so far as they
are used for such purposes, come under the ban
of either morality or religion. Therein we have, I
suggest, the reason of a certain confusion of thought

in the minds of students of the science of religion. We of the present day look at the means employed. We see the same means employed for ends that are, and for ends that are not, antisocial; and, inasmuch as the means are the same and are alike irrational, we group them all together under the head of magic. The grouping is perfectly correct, inasmuch as the proceedings grouped together have the common attribute of being proceedings which cannot possibly produce the effects which those who employ them believe that they will and do produce. But this grouping becomes perfectly misleading, if we go on to infer, as is sometimes inferred, that primitive man adopted it. First, it is based on the fact that the proceedings are uniformly irrational — a fact of which man is at first wholly unaware; and which, when it begins to dawn upon him, presents itself in the form of the further error that while some of these proceedings are absurd, others are not. In neither case does he adopt the modern, scientific position that all are irrational, impossible, absurd. Next, the modern position deals only with the proceedings as means, — declaring them all absurd, — and overlooks entirely what is to primitive man the point of fundamental importance, viz. the object and purpose with which they are used. Yet it is the object and purpose which determine the social value of these proceedings. For him, or in his eyes, to class together the things which he approves of and the things of which he disapproves would be monstrous: the means employed in the two cases may be the same, but that is of no importance in face of the fact that the ends aimed at in the two cases are not merely different but contradictory. In the one case the object promotes the common weal, or is supposed by him to promote it. In the other it is destructive of the common weal.

If, therefore, we wish to avoid confusion of thought, we must in discussing magic constantly bear in mind that we group together — and therefore are in danger of confusing — things which to the savage differ *toto caelo* from one another. A step towards avoiding this confusion is taken by Dr. Frazer, when he distinguishes (*History of the Kingship*, p. 89) between private magic and public magic. The distinction is made still more emphatic by Dr. Haddon (*Magic and Fetichism*, p. 20) when he speaks of "nefarious magic." The very same means when employed against the good of the community are regarded, by morality and religion alike, as nefarious, which when employed for the good of the community are regarded with approval. The very same illegitimate application, — I mean logically illegitimate in our eyes, — the very same application of the principle that like produces like will be condemned by the public opinion of the community when it is employed for purposes of murder and praised by public opinion when it is employed to produce the rain which the community desires. The distinction drawn by primitive man between the two cases is that, though any one can use the means to do either, no one ought to do the one which the community condemns. That is condemned as nefarious; and because it is nefarious, the "witch" may be "smelled out" by the "witch-doctor" and destroyed by, or with the approval of, the community.

But though that is, I suggest, the first stage in the process by which the belief in magic is evolved, it is by no means the whole of the process. Indeed, it may fairly be urged that practices which any one can perform, though no one ought to perform, may be nefarious (as simple, straightforward murder is), but so far there is nothing magical about them. And I am prepared to accept that view. Indeed, it is an essential part of my argument, for I seek to show that the belief in magic had a beginning and was evolved out of something that was not a belief in magic, though it gave rise to it. The belief that like produces like can be entertained where magic has not so much as been heard of. And, though it may ultimately be worked out into the scientific position that the sum of conditions necessary to produce an effect is indistinguishable from the effect, it may also be worked out on other lines into a belief in magic; and the first step in that evolution is taken when the belief that like produces like is used for purposes pronounced by public opinion to be nefarious.

The next step is taken when it comes to be believed not only that the thing is nefarious but that not every one can do it. The reason why only a certain person can do it may be that he alone knows how to do it — or he and the person from whom he learnt it. The lore of such persons when examined by folk-lore students is found generally to come under one or other of the two classes known as sympathetic and mimetic magic, or homœopathic and contagious magic. In these cases it is obvious that the *modus operandi* is the same as it was in what I have called the first stage in the evolution of magic and have already described at great length. What differentiates this second stage from the first is that whereas in the first stage these applications of the principle that like produces like are known to every one, though not practised by every one, in the second stage these applications are not known to every one, but only to the dealers in magic. Some of those applications of the principle may be applications which have descended to the dealer and have passed out of the general memory; and others may simply be extensions of the principle which have been invented by the dealer or his teacher. Again, the public disapproval of nefarious arts will tend first to segregate the followers of such arts from the rest of the community; and next to foster the notion that the arts thus segregated, and thereby made more or less mysterious, include not only things which the ordinary decent member of society would not do if he could, but also things which he could not do if he would. The mere belief in the possibility of such arts creates an atmosphere of suspicion in which things are believed because they are impossible. When this stage has been reached, when he who practises nefarious arts is reported and believed to do things which ordinary decent people could not do if they would, his personality inevitably comes to be considered as a factor in the results that he produces; he is credited with a power to produce them which other people, that is to say ordinary people, do not possess. And it is that personal power which eventually comes to be the most important, because the most mysterious, article in his equipment. It is in virtue of that personal power that he is commonly believed to be able to do things which are impossible for the ordinary member of the tribe.

Thus far I have been tracing the steps of the process by which the worker of nefarious arts starts by employing for nefarious purposes means which any one could use if he would, and ends by being credited with a power peculiar to himself of working impossibilities. I now wish to point out that a process exactly parallel is simultaneously carried on by which arts beneficent to society are supposed to be evolved. Rain-making may be taken as an art socially beneficial. The *modus operandi* of rain-making appears in all cases to be based on the principle that like produces like; and to be in its nature a process which any one can carry out and which requires no mysterious art to effect and no mysterious personal power to produce. At the same time, as it is a proceeding which is beneficial to the tribe as a whole, it is one in which the whole tribe, and no one tribesman in particular, is interested. It must be carried out in the interest of the tribe and by some one who in carrying it out acts for the tribe. The natural representative of the tribe is the head-man of the tribe; and, though any one might perform the simple actions necessary, and could perform them just as well as the head-man, they tend to fall into the hands of the head-man; and in any case the person who performs them performs them as the representative of the tribe. The natural inference comes in course of time to be drawn that he who alone performs them is the man who alone can perform them; and when that inference is drawn it becomes obvious that his personality, or the power peculiar to him personally, is necessary if rain is to be made, and that the acts and ceremonies through which he goes and through which any one could go would not be efficacious, or not as efficacious, without his personal agency and mysterious power. Hence the man who works wonders for his tribe or in the interests of his tribe, in virtue of his personal power, does things which are impossible for the ordinary member of the tribe.

Up to this point, in tracing the evolution of magic, we have not found it once necessary to bring in or even to refer to any belief in the existence of spiritual beings of any kind. So far as the necessities of the argument are concerned, the belief in magic might have originated in the way I have described and might have developed on the lines suggested, in a tribe which had never so much as heard of spirits. Of course, as a matter of fact, every tribe in which the belief in magic is found does also believe in the existence of spirits; animism is a stage of belief lower than which or back of which science does not profess to go. But it is only in an advanced stage of its evolution that the belief in magic becomes involved with the belief in spirits. Originally, eating tiger to make you bold, or eating saffron to cure jaundice, was just as matter of fact a proceeding as drinking water to moisten your throat or sitting by a fire to get warm; like produces like, and beyond that obvious fact it was not necessary to go — there was no more need to imagine that the action of the saffron was due to a spirit than to imagine that it was a water spirit which slakes your thirst. The fact seems to be that animism is a savage philosophy which is competent to explain everything when called upon, but that the savage does not spend every moment of his waking life in invoking it: until there is some need to fall back upon it, he goes on treating inanimate things as things which he can utilise for his own purposes without reference to spirits. That is the attitude also of the man who in virtue of his lore or his personal power can produce effects which the ordinary man cannot or will not: he performs his ceremony and the effect follows — or will follow — because he knows how to do it or has mysterious personal power to produce the effect. But he consults no spirits — at any rate in the first instance. Eventually he may do so; and then magic enters on a further stage in its evolution. (See Appendix.)

If the man who has the lore or the personal power, and who uses it for nefarious purposes, proposes to employ it on obtaining the same control over spirits as he has over things, his magic reaches a stage of evolution in which it is difficult and practically unnecessary to distinguish it from the stage of fetichism in which the owner of a fetich applies coercion to make the fetich spirit do what he wishes. With fetichism I deal in another lecture.

If, on the other hand, the man who has the lore or the personal power and uses it for social or "communal" purposes (Haddon, p. 41) comes to believe that, for the effects which he has hitherto sought to produce by means of his superior knowledge or superior power, it is necessary to invoke the aid of spirits, he will naturally address himself to the spirit or god who is worshipped by the community because he has at heart the general interests of the community; or it may be that the spirit who produces such a benefit for the community at large, as rain for example, will take his place among the gods of the community as the rain-god, in virtue of the benefit which he confers upon the community generally. In either case, the attitude of the priest or person who approaches him on behalf of the community will be that which befits a supplicant invoking a favour from a power that has shown favour in the past to the community. And it will not surprise us if we find that the ceremonies which were used for the purpose of rain-making, before rain was recognised as the gift of the gods, continue for a time to be practised as the proper rites with which to approach the god of the community or the rain-god in particular. Such survivals are then in danger of being misinterpreted by students of the science of religion, for they may be regarded as evidence that religion was evolved out of magic, when in truth they show that religion tends to drive out magic. Thus Dr. Frazer, in his *Lectures on the Early History of the Kingship* (pp. 73–75), describes the practice of the New Caledonians who, to promote the growth of taro, "bury in the field certain stones resembling taros, praying to their ancestors at the same time," and he goes on to say: "In these practices of the New Caledonians the magical efficacy of the stones appears to be deemed insufficient of itself to accomplish the end in view; it has to be reinforced by the spirits of the dead, whose help is sought by prayer and sacrifice. Thus in New Caledonia sorcery is blent with the worship of the dead; in other words, magic is combined with religion. If the stones ceased to be employed, and the prayers and sacrifices to the ancestors remained, the transition from magic to religion would be complete." Thus it seems to be suggested in these words of Dr. Frazer's that religion may be evolved out of magic. If that is what is suggested, then there is little doubt that the suggestion is not borne out by the instance given. Let us concede for the moment what some of us would be inclined to doubt, viz. that prayers and sacrifice offered to a human being, alive or dead, is religion; and let us enquire whether this form of religion is evolved out of magic. The magic here is quite clear: stones resembling taros are buried in the taro field to promote the growth of taros. That is an application of the principle that like produces like which might be employed by men who had never heard of ancestor worship or of any kind of religion, and who had never uttered prayers or offered sacrifices of any kind. Next, the religious element, according to Dr. Frazer, is also quite clear: it consists in offering sacrifices to the dead with the prayer or the words, "Here are your offerings, in order that the crop of yams may be good." Now, it is not suggested, even by Dr. Frazer, that this religious element is a form of magic or is in any way developed out of or evolved from magic. On the contrary, if this element is religious — indeed, whether it be really religious or not — it is obviously entirely distinct and different from sympathetic or homœopathic magic. The mere fact that the magical

rite of burying in the taro fields stones which resemble taros has to be supplemented by rites which
are, on Dr. Frazer's own showing, non-magical,
shows that the primitive belief in this application
of the principle that like produces like was already
dying out, and was in process of becoming a mere
survival. Suppose that it died out entirely and
the rite of burying stones became an unintelligible
survival, or was dropped altogether, and suppose
that the prayers and sacrifices remained in possession
of the field, which would be the more correct way
of stating the facts, to say that the magic had died
out and its place had been taken by something
totally different, viz. religion; or that what was
magic had become religion, that magic and religion
are but two manifestations, two stages, in the evolution of the same principle? The latter statement
was formally rejected by Dr. Frazer in the second
edition of his *Golden Bough*, when he declared that
he had come to recognise "a fundamental distinction and even opposition of principle between magic
and religion" (Preface, xvi). His words, therefore,
justify us in assuming that when he speaks, in his
Lectures on the Early History of the Kingship, of
the "transition from magic to religion," he cannot

mean that magic becomes religion, or that religion is evolved out of magic, for the "distinction and even opposition of principle" between the two is "fundamental." He can, therefore, only mean that magic is followed and may be driven out by something which is fundamentally opposed to it, viz. religion.

What then is the fundamental opposition between magic and religion? and is it such as to require us to believe with Dr. Frazer that magic preceded religion, and that of two opposite ideas the mind can conceive the one without conceiving — and rejecting — the other?

The fundamental opposition between magic and religion I take to be that religion is supposed to promote the interests of the community, and that magic, so far forth as it is nefarious, is condemned by the moral and by the religious feeling of the community. It is the ends for which nefarious magic is used that are condemned, and not the means. The means may be and, as we see, are silly and futile; and, for intellectual progress, their silliness and futility must be recognised by the intellect. But, it is only when they are used for purposes inimical to the public good that they are condemned by religion and morality as nefarious. If therefore we talk of a fundamental opposition between magic and religion, we must understand that the fundamental opposition is that between nefarious magic and religion; neither religion nor morality condemns the desire to increase the food supply or to promote any other interest of the community. Whether a man uses skill that he has acquired, or personal power, or force of will, matters not, provided he uses it for the general good. The question whether, as a cold matter of fact, the means he uses are efficacious is not one which moral fervour or religious ardour is competent by itself to settle: the cool atmosphere and dry light of reason have rather that function to perform; and they have to perform it in the case both of means that are used for the general good and of those used against it.

I take it therefore that what religion is fundamentally opposed to is magic — or anything else — that is used for nefarious purposes.

The question then arises whether we have any reason to believe that magic used for nefarious purposes must have existed before religion. Now by nefarious purposes I mean purposes inconsistent with or destructive of the common good.

There can be no such purposes, however, unless and until there is a community, however small, having common interests and a common good. As soon as there exists such a community, there will be a distinction between actions which promote and actions which are destructive of the common good. The one class will be approved, the other disapproved, of by public opinion. Magic will be approved and disapproved of according as it is or is not used in a way inconsistent with the public good. If there is a spirit or a god who is worshipped by the community because he is believed to be concerned with the good of the community, then he will disapprove of nefarious proceedings whether magical or not. But Dr. Frazer's position I take to be that no such spirit or god can come to be believed in, unless there has been previously a belief in magic. Now, that argument either is or is not based on the assumption that magic and religion are but two manifestations, two stages, in the evolution of the same principle. If that is the basis, then what manifested itself at first as magic subsequently manifests itself as religion; and "the transition from magic to religion" implies the priority of magic to religion. But, as we have seen, Dr. Frazer formally postulates, not an identity, but an "opposition of principle" between the two. We must therefore reject the assumption of an identity of principle; and accept the "opposition of principle." But if so, then there must be two principles which are opposed to one another, religion and magic; and we might urge that line of argument consistently enough to show that there can be no magic save where there is religion to be opposed to it.

Now, there is an opposition of principle between magic used for nefarious purposes and religion; and the opposition is that the one promotes social and the other anti-social purposes. Nefarious purposes, whether worked by magic or by other means, are condemned by religion and are nefarious especially because offensive to the god who has the interests of the community at heart. That from the moment society existed anti-social tendencies also manifested themselves will not be doubted; and neither need we doubt that the principle that like produces like was employed from the beginning for social as well as for anti-social purposes. The question is whether, in the stage of animism, the earliest and the lowest stage which science recognises in the evolution of man, there is ever found a society of human beings which has not appropriated some one or more of the spirits by which all things, on the animistic principle, are worked, to the purposes of the community. No such society has yet been proved to exist; still less has any *a priori* proof been produced to show that such a society must have existed. The presumption indeed is rather the other way. Children go through a period of helpless infancy longer than the young of any other creatures; and could not reach the age of self-help, if the family did not hold together for some years at least. But where there is a family there is a society, even if it be confined to members of the family. There also, therefore, there are social and anti-social tendencies and purposes; and, in the animistic stage, the spirits, by which man conceives himself to be surrounded, are either hostile or not hostile to the society, and are accordingly either worshipped or not worshipped by it. Doubtless, even in those early times, the father and the husband conceived himself to be the whole family; and if that view had its unamiable side — and it still has — it also on occasion had the inestimable advantage of sinking self, of self-sacrifice, in defence of the family.

Thus far I have been concerned to show how, starting from a principle such as that like produces like, about which there is nothing magical in the eyes either of those who believe in magic or of those who have left the belief behind, man might evolve the conception of magic as being the lore or the personal power which enables a man to do what ordinary people cannot do. A few words are necessary as to the decline of the belief. The first is that the belief is rotten before it is ripe. Those applications of the principle that like produces like which are magical are generally precisely those which are false. The fact that they are false has not prevented them from surviving in countless numbers to the present day. But some suspicion of their falsity in some cases does arise; and the person who has the most frequent opportunities of discovering their falsity, the person on whose notice the discovery of their falsity is thrust most pointedly, is the person who deals habitually and professionally in magic. Hence, though it is his profession to work wonders, he takes care as far as may be not to attempt impossibilities. Thus Dr. Haddon (*l.c.*, p. 62) found that the men of Murray Island, Torres Straits, who made a "big wind" by magic, only made it in the

season of the southeast trade wind. "On my asking," he says, "whether the ceremony was done in
the north monsoon, my informant said emphatically,
'Can't do it in northwest.' That is, the charm is
performed only at that season of the year when the
required result is possible — indeed when it is of
normal occurrence. In this, as in other cases, I
found that the impossible was never attempted. A
rain charm would not be made when there was no
expectation of rain coming, or a southeast wind be
raised during the wrong season." The instance
thus given to us by Dr. Haddon shows how the
belief in magic begins to give way before the scientific observation of fact. The collapse of magic
becomes complete when every one sees that the
southeast trade wind blows at its appointed time,
whether the magic rites are performed or not. In
fine, what kills magic regarded as a means for producing effects is the discovery that it is superfluous,
when for instance the desired wind or rain is coming,
and futile when it is not. And whereas morality and
religion only condemn the end aimed at by magic,
and only condemn it when it is anti-social, science
slowly shows that magic as a means to any end is
superfluous and silly.

Science, however, shows this but slowly; and if we wish to understand how it is that the belief in the magician's power has survived for thousands of years down to the present moment amongst numerous peoples, we must remember that his equipment and apparatus are not limited to purely nonsensical notions. On the contrary, in his stock of knowledge, carefully handed down, are many truths and facts not generally known; and they are the most efficacious articles of his stock in trade. Dr. Frazer may not go farther than his argument requires, but he certainly goes farther than the facts will support him, when he says (*l.c.*, p. 83) "for it must always be remembered that every single profession and claim put forward by the magician as such is false; not one of them can be maintained without deception, conscious or unconscious."

If now, in conclusion, we look once more at the subject of magic and look at it from the practical point of view of the missionary, we shall see that there are several conclusions which may be of use to him. In the first place, his attitude to magic will be hostile, and in his hostility to it he will find the best starting-point for his campaign against it to be in the fact that everywhere magic is felt, to a greater or less extent, to be anti-social, and is condemned both by the moral sentiments and the religious feeling of the community. It is felt to be essentially wicked; and in warring against it the missionary will be championing the cause of those who know it to be wrong but who simply dare not defy it. The fact that defiance is not ventured on is essential to the continuance of the tyranny; and what is necessary, if it is to be defied, is an actual concrete example of the fact that when defied it is futile.

Next, where magic is practised for social purposes, where it mimics science or religion and survives in virtue of its power of "protective colouring," it is in fact superfluous and silly; and where the natives themselves are beginning to recognise that the magic which is supposed, for instance, to raise the southeast trade wind won't act at the wrong season, it should not be difficult to get them to see that it is unnecessary at the right season. The natural process which tends thus to get rid of magic may be accelerated by the sensible missionary; and some knowledge of science will be found in this, as in other matters, an indispensable part of his training.

Finally, the missionary may rest assured in the conviction that his flank will not be turned by the science of religion. The idea that religion was preceded by and evolved out of magic may have been entertained by some students of the science of religion in the past, and may not yet have been thrown off by all. But it holds no place now in the science of religion. To derive either science or religion from the magic which exists only by mimicking one or the other is just as absurd as to imagine that the insect which imitates the colour of the leaf whereon it lives precedes and creates the tree which is to support it.

FETICHISM

THE line of action taken by the missionary at work will, like that of any other practical man, be conditioned, not only by the object which he wishes to attain, but also by the nature of the material on which and with which he has to work. He requires therefore all the information which the science of religion can place at his disposal about the beliefs and practices of those amongst whom his work is cast; and, if he is to make practical use of that information, he must know not only that certain beliefs and practices do as a matter of fact obtain, he must know also what is their value for his special purpose — what, if any, are the points about them which have religious value, and can be utilized by him; and what are those points about them which are obstructive to his purpose, and how best they may be removed and counteracted. To supply him with this information, to give him this estimate of values, to guide him as to the attitude he should assume and the way in which he may utilise or must

attack native practices and beliefs, is the object
with which the applied science of religion, when it
has been constituted by the action of Hartford
Theological Seminary, will address itself.

Now, it may seem from the practical point of view
of the missionary that with regard to fetichism
there can be no question as to what its value is or
as to what his attitude should be towards it. But,
even if we should ultimately find that fetichism is
obstructive to religion, we shall still want to know
what hints we can extract from the science of
religion as to the best way of cutting at the roots of
fetichism; and therefore it will be necessary to consider what exactly fetichism is. And, as a matter of
fact, there is a tendency manifesting itself amongst
students of the science of religion to say, as Dr.
Haddon says (*Magic and Fetichism*, p. 91), that
"fetichism is a stage of religious development";
and amongst writers on the philosophy of religion
to take fetichism and treat it, provisionally at any
rate, if not as the primitive religion of mankind, then
as that form of religion which "we find amongst
men at the lowest stage of development known to
us" (Höffding, *Philosophy of Religion*, E. T., §§ 45,
46). If, then, fetichism is the primitive religion of

mankind or a stage of religious development, "a basis from which many other modes of religious thought have been developed" (Haddon, p. 91), it will have a value which the missionary must recognise. And in any case he must know what value, if any, it has.

Now, if we are, I will not say to do justice to the view that fetichism is the primitive religion of mankind or a stage from which other modes of religious thought have been developed, but if we are simply to understand it, we must clearly distinguish it from the view — somewhat paradoxical to say the least — that fetichism has no religious value, and yet is the source of all religious values. The inference which may legitimately be drawn from this second view is that all forms of religious thought, having been evolved from this primitive religion of mankind, have precisely the same value as it has; they do but make explicit what it really was; the history of religion does but write large and set out at length what was contained in it from the first; in fetichism we see what from the first religion was, and what at the last religion is. On this view, the source from which all religious values spring is fetichism; fetichism has no value of any kind, and therefore the

evolved forms of fetichism which we call forms of
religion have no value either of any kind. Thus,
science — the science of religion — is supposed to
demonstrate by scientific methods the real nature
and the essential character of all religion.

Now, the error in this reasoning proceeds partly
on a false conception of the object and method of
science — a false conception which is slowly but
surely disappearing. The object of all science,
whether it be physical science or other, whether it
be historic science or other, is to establish facts.
The object of the historic science of religion is to
record the facts of the history of religion in such a
way that the accuracy of the record as a record will
be disputed by no one qualified to judge the fact.
For that purpose, it abstains deliberately and consistently from asking or considering the religious
value of any of the facts with which it deals. It has
not to consider, and does not consider, what would
have been, still less what ought to have been, the
course of history, but simply what it was. In this
it is following merely the dictates of common sense;
before we can profitably express an opinion on any
occurrence, we must know what exactly it was that
occurred; and to learn what occurred we must

divest our minds of preconceptions. It is the business of the science of religion to set aside preconceptions as to whether religion has or has not any value; and if it does set them aside, that is to say so far as it is scientific, it will end as it began without touching on the question of the value of religion. In fine, it is, and would I think now be generally admitted to be, a misconception of the function of the science of religion to imagine that it does, or can, prove anything as to the truth of religion, one way or the other.

There is, however, another error in the reasoning which is directed to show that in fetichism we see what religion was and essentially is. That error consists not only in a false conception of what religion is, — the man who has himself no religion may be excused if he fails to understand fully what it is, — it is based on a misunderstanding of what fetichism is. And so confusion is doubly confounded. The source of that misunderstanding is to be found in Bosman (Pinkerton, *Voyages and Travels*, London, 1814, XVI, 493), who says: "I once asked a negro with whom I could talk very freely . . . how they celebrated their divine worship, and what number of gods they had; he, laughing, answered that I had puzzled him; and assured me that nobody in the whole country could give me an exact account of it. 'For, as for my own part, I have a very large number of gods, and doubt not but that others have as many. For any of us being resolved to undertake anything of importance, we first of all search out a god to prosper our designed undertaking; and going out of doors with the design, take the first creature that presents itself to our eyes, whether dog, cat, or the most contemptible creature in the world for our god; or, perhaps, instead of that, any inanimate that falls in our way, whether a stone, a piece of wood, or anything else of the same nature. This new-chosen god is immediately presented with an offering, which is accompanied by a solemn vow, that if it pleaseth him to prosper our undertakings, for the future we will always worship and esteem him as a god. If our design prove successful, we have discovered a new and assisting god, which is daily presented with a fresh offering; but if the contrary happen, the new god is rejected as a useless tool, and consequently returns to his primitive estate. We make and break our gods daily, and consequently are the masters and inventors of what we sacrifice to.'" Now, all this was said by the

negro, as Bosman himself observed, to "ridicule his
own country gods." And it is not surprising that it
should have been, or should be, accepted as a trust-
worthy description of the earliest form of religion by
those who in the highest form can find no more than
this negro found in fetichism when he wished to
ridicule it.

Let us hold over for the moment the question
whether fetichism is or is not a form of religion;
and let us enquire how far the account given by Bosman's negro accords with the facts. First, though
there is no doubt that animals are worshipped as
gods, and though there is no doubt that the guardian
spirits of individuals are chosen, or are supposed to
manifest themselves, for example, amongst the North
American Indians, in animal form, and that "the
first creature that presents itself" to the man seeking the manifestation of his guardian spirit may be
taken to be his god, even though it be "the most
contemptible creature in the world"; still students of
the science of religion are fairly satisfied that such
gods or guardian spirits are not to be confused with
fetiches. A fetich is an inanimate or lifeless object,
even if it is the feather, claw, bone, eyeball, or any
other part of an animal or even of a man. It is as

Bosman's negro said, "any inanimate that falls in our way." When he goes on to say that it "is immediately presented with an offering," and, so long as its owner believes in it, "is daily presented with a fresh offering," he is stating a fact that is beyond dispute, and which is fully recognised by all students. A typical instance is given by Professor Tylor (*Primitive Culture*, II, 158) of the owner of a stone which had been taken as a fetich: "He was once going out on important business, but crossing the threshold he trod on this stone and hurt himself. Ha! ha! thought he, art thou there? So he took the stone, and it helped him through his undertaking for days." When Bosman's negro further goes on to state that if the fetich is discovered by its owner not to prosper his undertakings, as he expected it to do, "it is rejected as a useless tool," he makes a statement which is admitted to be true and which, in its truth, may be understood to mean that when the owner finds that the object is not a fetich, he casts it aside as being nothing but the "inanimate" which it is. Bosman's negro, however, says not that the inanimate but that "the new god is rejected as a useless tool." That we must take as being but a carelessness of expression; the evidence of Colonel

Ellis, an observer whose competence is undoubted, is: "Every native with whom I have conversed on the subject has laughed at the possibility of it being supposed that he could worship or offer sacrifice to some such object as a stone, which of itself would be perfectly obvious to his senses was a stone only and nothing more" (*The Tshi-speaking Peoples*, p. 192). From these words it follows that the object worshipped as a fetich is a stone (or whatever it is) and something more, and that the object "rejected as a useless tool" is a stone (or whatever it is) and nothing more. When, then, Bosman's negro goes on to say, "we make and break our gods daily," he is not describing accurately the processes as they are conceived by those who perform them. The fetich worshipper believes that the object which arrests his attention has already the powers which he ascribes to it; and it is in consequence of that belief that he takes it as his fetich. And it is only when he is convinced that it is not a fetich that he rejects it as a useless tool. But what Bosman's negro suggests, and apparently intended to suggest, is that the fetich worshipper makes, say, a stone his god, knowing that it is a stone and nothing more; and that he breaks his fetich believing it to be a god.

Thus the worshipper knows that the object is no god when he is worshipping it; but believes it to be a god when he rejects it as a useless tool. Now that is, consciously or unconsciously, deliberately or not, a misrepresentation of fetichism; and it is precisely on that misconception of what fetichism is that they base themselves who identify religion with fetichism, and then argue that, as fetichism has no value, religious or reasonable, neither has religion itself.

Returning now to the question what fetichism is — a question which must be answered before we can enquire what religious value it possesses, and whether it can be of any use for the practical purposes of the missionary in his work — we have now seen that a fetich is not merely an "inanimate," but something more; and that an object to become regarded as a fetich must attract the attention of the man who is to adopt it, and must attract the attention of the man when he has business on hand, that is to say when he has some end in view which he desires to attain, or generally when he is in a state of expectancy. The process of choice is one of "natural selection." Professor Höffding sees in it "the simplest conceivable construction of religious ideas. The choice is entirely elementary

and involuntary, as elementary and involuntary as
the exclamation which is the simplest form of a
judgment of worth. The object chosen must be
something or other which is closely bound up
with whatever engrosses the mind. It perhaps
awakens memories of earlier events in which
it was present or coöperative, or else it presents a certain — perhaps a very distant — similarity
to objects which helped in previous times of need.
Or it may be merely the first object which presents
itself in a moment of strained expectation. It
attracts attention, and is therefore involuntarily
associated with what is about to happen, with the
possibility of attaining the desired end" (*Philosophy
of Religion*, E. T., p. 139). And then Professor
Höffding goes on to say, "In such phenomena as
these we encounter religion under the guise of desire." Now, without denying that there are such
things as religious desires — and holding as we do
that religion is the search after God and the yearning of the human heart after Him, "the desire
of all nations," we shall have no temptation to
deny that there are such things as religious desires
— yet we must for the moment reserve our decision
on the question whether it is in such phenomena

as these that we encounter religious desires, and we must bear in mind that there are desires which are not religious, and that we want to know whether it is in the phenomena of fetichism that we encounter religious desires.

That in the phenomena of fetichism we encounter desires other than religious is beyond dispute: the use of a fetich is, as Dr. Nassau says, "to aid the possessor in the accomplishment of some specific wish" (*Fetichism in West Africa*, p. 82); that is, of any specific wish. Now, a fetich is, as we have seen, an inanimate object and something more. What more? In actual truth, nothing more than the fact that it is "involuntarily associated with what is about to happen, with the possibility of attaining the desired end." But to the possessor the something more, it may be said, is the fact that it is not merely an "inanimate" but also a spirit, or the habitation of a spiritual being. When, however, we reflect that fetichism goes back to the animistic stage of human thought, in which all the things that we term inanimate are believed to be animated by spirits, it is obvious that we require some differentia to mark off those things (animated by spirits) which are fetiches from those things (animated by spirits) which are not. And the differentia is, of course, that fetiches are spirits, or objects animated by spirits, which will aid the possessor in the accomplishment of some specific wish, and are thought to be willing so to aid, owing to the fact that by an involuntary association of ideas they become connected in the worshipper's mind with the possibility of attaining the end he has in view at the moment.

To recognise fetichism, then, in its simplest if not in its most primitive form, all we need postulate is animism — the belief that all things are animated by spirits — and the process of very natural selection which has already been described. At this stage in the history of fetichism it is especially difficult to judge whether the fetich is the spirit or the object animated by the spirit. As Dr. Haddon says (p. 83), " Just as the human body and soul form one individual, so the material object and its occupying spirit or power form one individual, more vague, perhaps, but still with many attributes distinctively human. It possesses personality and will . . . it possesses most of the human passions, — anger, revenge, also generosity and gratitude; it is within reach of influence and may be benevolent, hence to be deprecated and placated, and its aid enlisted."

A more advanced stage in the history of fetichism is that which is reached by reflection on the fact that a fetich not unfrequently ceases to prosper the undertakings of its possessor in the way he expected it to do. On the principles of animism, everything that is — whether animate, or inanimate according to our notions — is made up of spirit, or soul, and body. In the case of man, when he dies, the spirit leaves the body. When, therefore, a fetich ceases to act, the explanation by analogy is that the spirit has left the body, the inanimate, with which it was originally associated; and when that is the case, then, as we learn from Miss Kingsley (*Travels in West Africa*, pp. 304–305), "the little thing you kept the spirit in is no more use now, and only fit to sell to a white man as 'a big curio.'" The fact that, in native belief, what we call an inanimate thing may lose its soul and become really dead is shown by Miss Kingsley in a passage quoted by Dr. Haddon: "Everything that he," the native, "knows by means of his senses he regards as a twofold entity — part spirit, part not spirit, or, as we should say, matter; the connection of a certain spirit with a certain mass of matter, he holds, is not permanent. He will point out to you a lightning-struck tree, and tell you its spirit has been broken; he will tell you when the cooking-pot has been broken, that it has lost its spirit" (*Folk-Lore*, VIII, 141). We might safely infer then that as any object may lose its spirit, so too may an object which has been chosen as a fetich; even if we had not, as we have, direct testimony to the belief.

Next, when it is believed that an object may lose its spirit and become dead indeed, there is room and opportunity for the belief to grow that its spirit may pass into some other object: that there may be a transmigration of spirits. And when this belief arises, a fresh stage in the history of fetichism is evolved. And the fresh stage is evolved in accordance with the law that governs the whole evolution of fetichism. That law is that a fetich is an object believed to aid its possessor in attaining the end he desires. In the earliest stage of its history anything which happens to arrest a man's attention when he is in a state of expectancy "is involuntarily associated with what is about to happen," and so becomes a fetich. In the most developed stage of fetichism, men are not content to wait until they stumble across a fetich, and when they do so to say, "Ha! ha! art thou there?" Their mental attitude becomes in-

terrogative: "Ha! ha! where art thou?" They
no longer wait to stumble across a fetich, they proceed to make one; and for that procedure a belief
in the transmigration of spirits is essential. An
object, a habitation for the spirit, is prepared; and
he is invited, conjúred, or cónjured, into it. If he
is conjúred into it, the attitude of the man who
invites him is submissive; if cónjured, the mental
attitude of the performer is one of superiority.
Colonel Ellis throughout all his careful enquiries
found that "so great is the fear of giving possible
offence to any superhuman agent" that (in the region
of his observation) we may well believe that even the
makers of fetiches did not assume to command the
spirits. But elsewhere, in other regions, it is impossible to doubt but that the owners of fetiches
not only conjúre the spirits into the objects, but also
apply coercion to them when they fail to aid their
possessor in the accomplishment of his wishes.
That, I take it, is the ultimate stage in the evolution,
the fine flower, of fetichism. And it is not religion,
it has no value as religion, or rather its value is anti-
religious. Even if we were to accept as a definition
of religion that it is the conciliation of beings conceived to be superior, we should be compelled by

the definition to say that fetichism in its eventual outcome is not religion, for the attitude of the owner towards his fetich is then one of superiority, and his method is, when conciliation fails, to apply coercion.

But it may perhaps be argued that fetichism, except in what I have termed its ultimate evolution, is religion and has religious value; or, to put it otherwise, that what I have represented as the eventual outcome is really a perversion or the decline of fetichism. Then, in the fetichism which is or represents the primitive religion of mankind we meet, according to Professor Höffding, "religion under the guise of desire." Now, not all desires are religious; and the question, which is purely a question of fact, arises whether the desires which fetichism subserves are religious. And in using the word "religious" I will not here place any extravagant meaning on the word; I will take it in the meaning which would be understood by the community in which the owner of a fetich dwells himself. In the tribes described by Colonel Ellis, for instance, there are worshipped personal gods having proper names; and the worship is served by duly appointed priests; and the worshippers consist of a body of persons whose welfare the god has at heart. Such are some of the salient features of what all students of the science of religion would include under the head of the religion of those tribes. Now amongst those same tribes the fetich, or *suhman*, as it is termed by them, is found; and there are several features which make a fetich quite distinguishable from any of the gods which are worshipped there. Thus, the fetich has no body of worshippers: it is the private property of its owner, who alone makes offerings to it. Its *raison d'être*, its special and only function, is to subserve the private wishes of its owner. In so far as he makes offerings to it he may be called its priest; but he is not, as in the case of the priests of the gods who are worshipped there, the representative of the community or congregation, for a fetich has no plurality of worshippers; and none of the priests of the gods will have anything to do with it. Next, "though offerings are made to the *suhman* by its owner, they are made in private" (Jevons, *History of Religion*, p. 165) — there is no public worship — and "public opinion does not approve of them." The interests and the desires which the fetich exists to promote are not those of the community: they are antisocial, for, as Colonel Ellis tells us, "one of the special attributes of a *suhman* is to procure the death of any person whom its worshipper may wish to have removed" — indeed "the most important function of the *suhman* appears to be to work evil against those who have injured or offended its worshipper."

Thus, a very clear distinction exists between the worship of a fetich and the worship of the gods. It is not merely that the fetich is invoked occasionally in aid of antisocial desires: nothing can prevent the worshipper of a god, if the worshipper be bad enough, from praying for that which he ought not to pray for. It is that the gods of the community are there to sanction and further all desires which are for the good of the community, and that the fetich is there to further desires which are not for the good of the community, — hence it is that "public opinion does not approve of them." At another stage of religious evolution, it becomes apparent and is openly pronounced that neither does the god of the community approve of them; and then fetichism, like the sin of witchcraft, is stamped out more or less. But amongst the tribes who have only reached the point of religious progress attained by the natives of West Africa, public opinion has only gone so far as to express disapproval, not to declare war.

If, then, we are to hold to the view of Professor Höffding and of Dr. Haddon, that fetichism is in its essence, or was at the beginning, religious in its nature, though it may be perverted into something non-religious or anti-religious, we must at any rate admit that it has become non-religious not only in the case of those fetichists who assume an attitude of superiority and command to their fetiches, but also in the earlier stage of evolution when the fetichist preserves an attitude of submission and conciliation towards his fetich, but assumes the attitude only for the purpose of realising desires which are anti-social and recognised to be anti-religious.

But, if we take — as I think we must take — that line of argument, the conclusion to which it will bring us is fairly clear and is not far off. The differentia or rather that differentia which characteristically marks off the fetich from the god is the nature of the desires which each exists to promote; the function which each exists to fulfil, the end which is there for each to subserve. But the ends are different. Not only are they different, they are antagonistic. And the process of evolution does but bring out the antagonism, it does not create it. It was there from the beginning. From the moment there was society, there were desires which could only be realised at the cost and to the loss of society, as well as desires in the realisation of which the good of society was realised. The assistance of powers other than human might be sought; and the nature of the power which was sought was determined by the end or purpose for which its aid was employed or invoked — if for the good of society, it was approved by society; if not, not. Its function, the end it subserved, determined its value for society — determined whether public opinion should approve or disapprove of it, whether it was a god of the community or the fetich of an individual. Society can only exist where there is a certain community of purpose among its members; and can only continue to exist where anti-social tendencies are to some extent suppressed or checked by force of public opinion.

Fetichism, then, in its tendency and in its purpose, in the function which it performs and the end at which it aims is not only distinguishable from religion, it is antagonistic to it, from the earliest period of its history to the latest. Religion is social, an affair of the community; fetichism is anti-social, condemned by the community. Public opinion, expressing the moral sentiments of the community as well as its religious feeling, pronounces both moral and religious disapproval of the man who uses a *suhman* for its special purpose of causing death — committing murder. Fetichism is offensive to the morality as well as to the religion even of the native. To seek the origin of religion in fetichism is as vain as to seek the origin of morality in the selfish and self-seeking tendencies of man. There is no need to enquire whether fetichism is historically prior to religion, or whether religion is historically prior to fetichism. Man, as long as he has lived in societies, must have had desires which were incompatible with the welfare of the community as well as desires which promoted its welfare. The powers which are supposed to care whether the community fares well are the gods of the community; and their worship is the religion of the community. The powers which have no such care are not gods, nor is their worship — if coercion or cajolery can be called worship — religion. The essence of fetichism on its external side is that the owner of the fetich alone has access to it, alone can pray to it, alone can offer sacrifices to it. It is therefore in its inward essence directly destructive of the unity of interests and purposes that society demands and religion promotes. Perhaps it would be going too far to say that the practice of making prayers and offerings to a fetich is borrowed from religious worship: they are the natural and instinctive method of approaching any power which is capable of granting or refusing what we desire. It is the quarter to which they are addressed, and the end for which they are employed, that makes the difference between them. It is the fact that in the one case they are, and in the other are not, addressed to the quarter to which they ought to be addressed, and employed for the end for which they ought to be employed, that makes the difference in religious value between them.

If we bear in mind the simple fact that fetichism is condemned by the religious and moral feelings of the communities in which it exists, we shall not fall into the mistake of regarding fetichism either as the primitive religion of mankind or as a stage of religious development or as "a basis from which many other modes of religious thought have been developed."

Professor Höffding, holding that fetichism is the primitive religion, out of which polytheism was developed, adopts Usener's theory as to the mode of its evolution. "The fetich," Professor Höffding says (p. 140), "is only the provisional and momentary dwelling-place of a spirit. As Hermann Usener has strikingly called it, it is 'the god of a moment.'" But though Professor Höffding adopts this definition of a fetich, it is obvious that the course of his argument requires us to understand it as subject to a certain limitation. His argument in effect is that fetichism is not polytheism, but something different, something out of which polytheism was evolved. And the difference is that polytheism means a plurality of gods, whereas fetichism knows no gods, but only spirits. Inasmuch then as, on the theory — whether it is held by Höffding or by anybody else — that the spirits of fetichism become the gods of polytheism, there must be differences between the spirits of the one and the gods of the other, let us enquire what the differences are supposed to be.

First, there is the statement that a fetich is the "god of a moment," by which must be meant that the spirits which, so long as they are momentary and temporary, are fetiches, must come to be permanent if they are to attain to the rank of gods.

But on this point Dr. Haddon differs. He is quite clear that a fetich may be worshipped permanently without ceasing to be a fetich. And it is indeed abundantly clear that an object only ceases to be worshipped when its owner is convinced that it is not really a fetich; as long as he is satisfied that it is a fetich, he continues its cult — and he continues it because it is his personal property, because he, and not the rest of the community, has access to it.

Next, Höffding argues that it is from these momentary fetiches that special or specialised deities — "departmental gods," as Mr. Andrew Lang has termed them — arise. And these "specialised divinities constitute an advance on gods of the moment" (p. 142). Now, what is implied in this argument, what is postulated but not expressed, is that a fetich has only one particular thing which it can do. A departmental god can only do one particular sort of thing, has one specialised function. A departmental god is but a fetich advanced one stage in the hierarchy of divine beings. Therefore the function of the fetich in the first instance was specialised and limited.   But there it is that the *a priori* argument comes into collision with the actual facts. A fetich, when it presents itself to a man, assists him in the particular business on which he is at the moment engaged.   But it only continues to act as a fetich, provided that it assists him afterwards and in other matters also.   The desires of the owner are not limited, and consequently neither are his expectations; the business of the fetich is to procure him general prosperity (Haddon, p. 83).   As far as fetiches are concerned, it is simply reversing the facts to suppose that it is because one fetich can only do one thing, that many fetiches are picked up. Many objects are picked up on the chance of their proving fetiches, because if the object turns out really to be a fetich it will bring its owner good luck and prosperity generally—there is no knowing what it may do.   But it is only to its owner that it brings prosperity — not to other people, not to the community, for the community is debarred access to it.

The next difference between fetichism and polytheism, according to Höffding, is that the gods of polytheism have developed that personality which is not indeed absolutely wanting in the spirits of fetichism but can hardly be said to be properly there. "The transition," he says, "from momentary and special gods to gods which can properly be called personal is one of the most important transitions in the history of religion. It denotes the transition from animism to polytheism" (p. 145). And one of the outward signs that the transition has been effected is, as Usener points out with special emphasis, "that only at a certain stage of evolution, *i.e.*, on the appearance of polytheism, do the gods acquire proper names" (*ib.* 147).

Now, this argument, I suggest, seeks to make, or to make much of, a difference between fetichism and polytheism which scarcely exists, and so far as it does exist is not the real difference between them. It seeks to minimise, if not to deny, the personality of the fetich, in order to exalt that of the gods of polytheism. And then this difference in degree of personality, this transition from the one degree to the other, is exhibited as "one of the most important transitions in the history of religion." The question therefore is first whether the difference is so great, and next whether it is the real difference between fetichism and religion in the polytheistic stage.

The difference in point of personality between the spirits of fetichism and the gods of polytheism is not absolute. The fetich, according to Dr. Haddon, "*possesses personality* and will, it has also many human characters. It possesses most of the human passions, anger, revenge, also generosity and gratitude; it is within reach of influence and may be benevolent, is hence to be deprecated and placated, and its aid to be enlisted" (p. 83); "the fetich is worshipped, prayed to, sacrificed to, and talked with" (p. 89).

But, perhaps it may be said that, though the fetich does "possess personality," it is only when it has acquired sufficient personality to enjoy a proper name that it becomes a god, or fetichism passes into polytheism. To this the reply is that polytheism does not wait thus deferentially on the evolution of proper names. There was a period in the evolution of the human race when men neither had proper names of their own nor knew their fellows by proper names; and yet they doubted not their personality. The simple fact is that he who is to receive a name—whether he be a human being or a spiritual being—must be there in order to be named. When he is there he may receive a name which has lost all meaning, as proper names at the present day have generally done; or one which has a meaning.

A mother may address her child as "John" or as "boy," but, whichever form of address she uses, she has no doubt that the child has a personality. The fact that a fetich has not acquired a proper name is not a proof that it has acquired no personality; if it can, as Dr. Haddon says it can, be "petted or ill-treated with regard to its past or future behaviour" (p. 90), its personality is undeniable. If it can be "worshipped, prayed to, sacrificed to, talked with," it is as personal as any deity in a pantheon. If it has no proper name, neither at one time had men themselves. And Höffding himself seems disinclined to follow Usener on this point: "no important period," he says (p. 147), "in the history of religion can begin with an empty word. The word can neither be the beginning nor exist at the beginning."

Finally Höffding, to enforce the conclusion that polytheism is evolved from fetichism, says: "The influence exerted by worship on the life of religious ideas can find no more striking exemplification than in the word 'god' itself: when we study those etymologies of this word which, from the philological point of view, appear most likely to be correct, we find the word really means 'he to whom sacrifice is made,' or 'he who is worshipped'" (p. 148).

Professor Wilhelm Thomsen considers the first explanation the more probable: "In that case there would be a relationship between the root of the word '*gott*' and '*giessen*' (to pour), as also between the Greek χέειν, whose root χυ = the Sanskrit *hu*, from which comes *huta*, which means 'sacrificed,' as well as 'he to whom sacrifices are made'" (p. 396). Now, if "god" means either "he to whom sacrifice is made" or "he who is worshipped," we have only to enquire by whom the sacrifice is made or the worship paid, according to Professor Höffding, in order to see the value of this philological argument. A leading difference between a fetich and a god is that sacrifice is made and worship paid to the fetich by its owner, to the god by the community. Now this philological derivation of "god" throws no light whatever on the question by whom the "god" is worshipped; but the content of the passage which I have quoted shows that Professor Höffding himself here understands the worship of a god to be the worship paid by the community. If that is so, and if the function or a function of the being worshipped is to grant the desires of his worshippers, then the function of the being worshipped by the community is to grant the desires of the community.

And if that is the distinguishing mark or a distinguishing mark of a god, then the worship of a god differs *toto cœlo* from the worship paid to a fetich, whose distinguishing mark is that it is subservient to the anti-social wishes of its owner, and is not worshipped by the community. And it is just as impossible to maintain that a god is evolved out of a fetich as it would be to argue — indeed it is arguing — that practices destructive of society or social welfare have only to be pushed far enough and they will prove the salvation of society.

If in the animistic stage, when everything that is is worked by spirits, it is possible and desirable for the individual to gain his individual ends by the coöperation of some spirit, it is equally possible and more desirable for the community to gain the aid of a spirit which will further the ends for the sake of which the community exists. But those ends are not transient or momentary, neither therefore can the spirit who promotes them be a "momentary" god. And if we accept Höffding's description of the simplest and earliest manifestation of the religious spirit as being belief "in a power which cares whether he [man] has or has not experiences which he values," we must be careful to make it clear that the power worshipped by a community is worshipped because he is believed to care that the community should have the experiences which the community values. Having made that stipulation, we may accept Höffding's further statement (p. 147) that "even the momentary and special gods implied the existence of a personifying tendency and faculty"; for, although from our point of view a momentary god is a self-contradictory notion, we are quite willing to agree that this tendency to personification may be taken as primary and primitive: religion from the beginning has been the search after a power essentially personal. But that way of conceiving spiritual powers is not in itself distinctive of or confined to religion: it is an intellectual conception; it is the essence of animism, and animism is not religion. To say that an emotional element also must be present is true; but neither will that serve to mark off fetichism from religion. Fetichism also is emotional in tone: it is in hope that the savage picks up the thing that may prove to have the fetich power; and it is with fear that he recognises his neighbour's *suhman.* A god is not merely a power conceived of intellectually and felt emotionally to be a personal power from whom things may be hoped or feared; he must indeed be a personal power and be regarded with hope and fear, but it is by a community that he must be so regarded. And the community, in turning to such a power, worships him with sacrifice: a god is indeed he to whom sacrifice is made and worship paid by the community, with whose interests and whose morality — with whose good, in a word, he is from the beginning identified. "In the absence of experience of good as one of the realities of life, no one," Höffding says, "would ever have believed in the goodness of the gods"; and, we may add, it is as interested in and caring for the good of the community that the god of the community is worshipped. It is in the conviction that he does so care, that religious feeling is rooted; or, as Höffding puts it (p. 162), it is rooted in "the need to collect and concentrate ourselves, to resign ourselves, to feel ourselves supported and carried by a power raised above all struggle and opposition and beyond all change." There we have, implicit from the beginning, that communion with god, or striving thereafter, which is essential to worship. It is faith. It is rest. It is the heart's desire. And it is not fetichism, nor is fetichism it.

PRAYER

THE physician, if he is to do his work, must know both a healthy and a diseased body, or organ, when he sees it. He must know the difference between the two and the symptoms both of health and disease. Otherwise he is in danger of trying to cure an organ which is healthy already — in which case his remedies will simply aggravate the disease. That is obviously true of the physician who seeks to heal the body, and it is equally, if not so obviously, true of the physician who seeks to minister to a mind, or a soul, diseased. Now, the missionary will find that the heathen, to whom he is to minister, have the habit of prayer; and the question arises, What is to be his attitude towards it? He cannot take up the position that prayer is in itself a habit to be condemned; he is not there to eradicate the habit, or to uproot the tendency. Neither is he there to create the habit; it already exists, and the wise missionary will acknowledge its existence with thankfulness. His business is not to teach his flock to

pray, but <u>how to pray</u>, that is to say, for what and
to whom. But even if he thus wisely recognises
that prayer is a habit not to be created, but to be
trained by him, it is still possible for him to assume
rashly that it is simply impossible for a heathen ever
to pray for anything that is right, and therefore,
that it is a missionary's duty first to insist that
everything for which a savage or barbarian prays
must be condemned as essentially irreligious and
wicked. In that case, what will such a missionary, if sent to the Khonds of Orissa, say, when he
finds them praying thus: "We are ignorant of what
it is good to ask for. You know what is good for
us. Give it to us!"? Can he possibly say to his
flock, "All your prayers, all the things that you pray
for now, are wicked; and your only hope of salvation
lies in ceasing to pray for them"? If not, then he
must recognise the fact that it is possible for the
heathen to pray, and to pray for some things that
it is right to pray for. And he must not only recognise the fact, but he must utilise it. Nay! more, he
must not only recognise the fact if it chances to
force itself upon him, he must go out of his way
with the deliberate purpose of finding out what
things are prayed for. He will then find himself in

more intimate contact with the soul of the man than he can ever attain to in any other way; and he may then find that there are other things for which petitions are put up which could not be prayed for save by a man who had a defective or erroneous conception of Him who alone can answer prayer.

But it is a blundering, unbusinesslike way of managing things if the missionary has to go out to his work unprepared in this essential matter, and has to find out these things for himself — and perhaps not find them out at all. The applied science of religion should equip him in this respect; it should be able to take the facts and truths established by the science of religion and apply them to the purposes of the missionary. But it is a striking example of the youth and immaturity of the science of religion that no attempt has yet been made by it to collect the facts, much less to coördinate and state them scientifically. If a thing is clear, when we come to think of it, in the history of religion, it is that the gods are there to be prayed to: man worships them because it is on their knees that all things lie. It is from them that man hopes all things; it is in prayer that man expresses his hopes and desires. It is from his prayers that we should be able to find out

what the gods really are to whom man prays. What
is said about them in mythology — or even in theology — is the product of reflection, and is in many
cases demonstrably different from what is given in
consciousness at the moment when man is striving
after communion with the Highest. Yet it is from
mythology, or from the still more reflective and de-
liberative expression of ritual, of rites and ceremonies,
that the science of religion has sought to infer the
nature of the gods man worships. The whole apparatus of religion, rites and ceremonies, sacrifice and
altars, nature-worship and polytheism, has been in-
vestigated; the one thing overlooked has been the
one thing for the sake of which all the others exist,
the prayer in which man's soul rises, or seeks to rise,
to God.

The reason given by Professor Tylor (*Primitive
Culture*, II, 364) for this is not that the subject is
unimportant, but that it is so simple; "so simple
and familiar," he says, "is the nature of prayer
that its study does not demand that detail of fact and
argument which must be given to rites in comparison practically insignificant." Now, it is indeed the
case that things which are familiar may appear to be
simple; but it is also the case that sometimes things

are considered simple merely because they are familiar, and not because they are simple. The fact that they are not so simple as every one has assumed comes to be suspected when it is discovered that people take slightly different views of them. Such slightly different views may be detected in this case.

Professor Höffding holds that, in the lowest form in which religion manifests itself, "religion appears under the guise of desire," thus ranging himself on the side of an opinion mentioned by Professor Tylor (*op. cit.*, II, 464) that, as regards the religion of the lower culture, in prayer "the accomplishment of desire is asked for, but desire is as yet limited to personal advantage." Now, starting from this position that prayer is the expression of desire, we have only to ask, whose desire? that of the individual or that of the community? and we shall see that under the simple and familiar phrase of "the accomplishment of desire" there lurks a difference of view which may possibly widen out into a very wide difference of opinion. If we appeal to the facts, we may take as an instance a prayer uttered "in loud uncouth voice of plaintive, piteous tone" by one of the Osages to Wohkonda, the Master of Life: "Wohkonda, pity me, I am very poor; give me what I need; give me success against mine enemies, that I may avenge the death of my friends. May I be able to take scalps, to take horses!" etc. (Tylor, II, 365). So on the Gold Coast a negro in the morning will pray, "Heaven! grant that I may have something to eat this day" (*ib.*, 368), not "give us this day our daily bread"; or, raising his eyes to heaven, he will thus address the god of heaven: "God, give me to-day rice and yams, gold and agries, give me slaves, riches and health, and that I may be brisk and swift!" (*ib.*). On the other hand, John Tanner (*Narrative*, p. 46) relates that when Algonquin Indians were setting out in a fleet of frail bark canoes across Lake Superior, the chief addressed a prayer to the Great Spirit: "You have made this lake; and you have made us, your children; you can now cause that the water shall remain smooth while we pass over in safety." The chief, it will be observed, did not expressly call the Great Spirit "our Father," but he did speak of himself and his men as "your children." If we cross over to Africa, again, we find the Masai women praying thus; and be it observed that though the first person singular is used,

it is used by the chorus of women, and is plural in
effect: —

I

"My God, to thee alone I pray
   That offspring may to me be given.
Thee only I invoke each day,
   O morning star in highest heaven.
God of the thunder and the rain,
Give ear unto my suppliant strain.
Lord of the powers of the air,
To thee I raise my daily prayer.

II

"My God, to thee alone I pray,
   Whose savour is as passing sweet
As only choicest herbs display,
   Thy blessing daily I entreat.
Thou hearest when I pray to thee,
And listenest in thy clemency.
Lord of the powers of the air,
To thee I raise my daily prayer."
                    —Hollis, *The Masai*, p. 346.

When Professor Tylor says that by the savage
"the accomplishment of desire is asked for, but
desire is as yet limited to personal advantage," we
must be careful not to infer that the only advantage
a savage is capable of praying for is his own selfish
advantage. Professor Tylor himself quotes (II,

366) the following prayer from the war-song of a Delaware: —

> " O Great Spirit there above,
>   Have pity on my children
>   And my wife!
>   Prevent that they shall mourn for me!
>   Let me succeed in this undertaking,
>   That I may slay my enemy
>   And bring home the tokens of victory
>   To my dear family and my friends
>   That we may rejoice together. . . .
>   Have pity on me and protect my life,
>   And I will bring thee an offering."

Nor is it exclusively for their own personal advantage that the Masai women are concerned when they pray for the safe return of their sons from the wars: —

> " O thou who gavest, thou to whom we pray
>   For offspring, take not now thy gift away.
>   O morning star, that shinest from afar,
>   Bring back our sons in safety from the war."
>   — HOLLIS, p. 351.

Nor is it in a purely selfish spirit that the Masai women pray that their warriors may have the advantage over all their enemies: —

I

> ' O God of battles, break
>   The power of the foe.

Their cattle may we take,
Their mightiest lay low.

II

"Sing, O ye maidens fair,
For triumph o'er the foe.
This is the time for prayer
Success our arms may know.

III

"Morning and evening stars
That in the heavens glow,
Break, as in other wars,
The power of the foe.

IV

"O dweller, where on high
Flushes at dawn the snow,
O Cloud God, break, we cry,
The power of the foe."

—*Ib.*, p. 352.

Again, the rain that is prayed for by the Manganja
of Lake Nyassa is an advantage indeed, but one
enjoyed by the community and prayed for by the
community. They made offerings to the Supreme
Deity that he might give them rain, and "the
priestess dropped the meal handful by handful on
the ground, each time calling in a high-pitched voice,

'Hear thou, O God, and send rain!' and the assembled people responded, clapping their hands softly and intoning (they always intone their prayers), 'Hear thou, O God'" (Tylor, p. 368).

The appeal then to facts shows that it is with the desires of the community that the god of the community is concerned, and that it is by a representative of the community that those desires are offered up in prayer, and that the community may join in. The appeal to facts shows, also, that an individual may put up individual petitions, as when a Yebu will pray: "God in heaven protect me from sickness and death. God give me happiness and wisdom." But we may safely infer that the only prayers that the god of the community is expected to harken to are prayers that are consistent with the interests and welfare of the community.

From that point of view we must refuse to give more than a guarded assent to the "opinion that prayer appeared in the religion of the lower culture, but that in this its earlier stage it was unethical" (Tylor, 364). Prayer obviously does appear in the religion of the lower culture, but to say that it there is unethical is to make a statement which requires defining. The statement means what Professor Tylor expresses later on in the words: "It scarcely appears as though any savage prayer, authentically native in its origin, were ever directed to obtain moral goodness or to ask pardon for moral sin" (p. 373). But it might be misunderstood to mean that among savages it was customary or possible to pray for things recognised by the savage himself as wrong, and condemned by the community at large. In the first place, however, the god of the community simply as being the god of the community would not tolerate such prayers. Next, the range and extent of savage morality is less extensive than it is — or at any rate than it ought to be — in our day; and though we must recognise and at the right time insist upon the difference, that ought not to make us close our eyes to the fact that the savage does pray to do the things which savage morality holds it incumbent on him to do, for instance to fight bravely for the good of his wife, his children, and his tribe, to carry out the duty of avenging murder. And if he prays for wealth he also prays for wisdom; if he prays that his god may deliver him from sickness, that shows he is human rather than that he is a low type of humanity.

It would seem, then, that though in religions of low

culture we meet religion under the guise of desire,
we also find that religion makes a distinction between desires; there are desires which may be
expressed to the god of the community, and desires
which may not. Further, though it is in the heart
of a person and an individual that desire must originate, it does not follow that prayer originates in
individual desire. To say so, we must assume that
the same desire cannot possibly originate simultaneously in different persons. But that is a patently
erroneous assumption: in time of war, the desire
for victory will spring up simultaneously in the
hearts of all the tribe; in time of drought, the
prayer for rain will ascend from the hearts of all
the people; at the time of the sowing of seed a prayer
for "the kindly fruits of the earth" may be uttered
by every member of the community. Now it is
precisely these desires, which being desires must
originate in individual souls, yet being desires of
every individual in the community are the desires
of the community, that are the desires which take
the form of prayer offered by the community or its
representative to the god of the community. Anti-
social desires cannot be expressed by the community
or sanctioned by religion. Prayer is the essential

expression of true socialism; and the spirit which prompts it is and has always been the moving spirit of social progress.

Professor Tylor, noticing the "extreme development of mechanical religion, the prayer-mill of the Tibetan Buddhists," suggests that it "may perhaps lead us to form an opinion of large application in the study of religion and superstition; namely, that the theory of prayers may explain the origin of charms. Charm-formulæ," he says, "are in very many cases actual prayers, and as such are intelligible. Where they are mere verbal forms, producing their effect on nature and man by some unexplained process, may not they or the types they have been modelled on have been originally prayers, since dwindled into mystic sentences?" (*P. C.* II, 372–373). Now, if this suggestion of Professor Tylor's be correct, it will follow that as charms and spells are degraded survivals of prayer, so magic generally — of which charms and spells are but one department — is a degradation of religion. That in many cases charms and spells are survivals of prayer — formulæ from which all spirit of religion has entirely evaporated — all students of the science of religion would now admit. That prayers may

stiffen into traditional formulæ, and then become
vain repetitions which may actually be unintelligible
to those who utter them, and so be conceived to
have a force which is purely magical and a "nature
practically assimilated more or less to that of
charms" (*l.c.*), is a fact which cannot be denied.
But when once the truth has been admitted that
prayers may pass into spells, the possibility is suggested that it is out of spells that prayer has
originated. Mercury raised to a high temperature
becomes red precipitate; and red precipitate exposed
to a still greater heat becomes mercury again. Spells
may be the origin of prayers, if prayers show a
tendency to relapse into spells. That possibility fits
in either with the theory that magic preceded religion or still more exactly with the theory that
religion simply is magic raised, so to speak, to a
higher moral temperature. We have therefore to
consider the possibility that the process of evolution
has been from spell to prayer (R. R. Marett, *Folk-
Lore* XV, 2, pp. 132–166); and let us begin the
consideration by observing that the reverse passage—
from prayer to spell — is only possible on the condition that religion evaporates entirely in the process.
The prayer does not become a charm until the

religion has disappeared entirely from it: a charm therefore is that in which no religion is, and out of which consequently no religion can be extracted. If then, *per impossibile*, it could be demonstrated that there was a period in the history of mankind, when charms and magic existed, and religion was utterly unknown; if it be argued that the spirit of religion, when at length it breathed upon mankind, transformed spells into prayers—still all that would then be maintained is that spoken formulæ which were spells were followed by other formulæ which are the very opposite of spells. Must we not, however, go one step further and admit that one and the same form of words may be prayer and religion when breathed in one spirit, and vain repetition and mere magic when uttered in another? Let us admit that the difference between prayer and spell lies in the difference of the spirit inspiring them; and then we shall see that the difference is essential, fundamental, as little to be ignored as it is impossible to bridge.

The formula used by the person employing it to express his desire may or may not in itself suffice to show whether it is religious in intent and value. Thus in West Africa the women of Framin dance

and sing, "Our husbands have gone to Ashantee
land; may they sweep their enemies off the face
of the earth" (Frazer, *Golden Bough*,[2] I, 34). We
may compare the song sung in time of war by the
Masai women: "O God, to whom I pray for offspring, may our children return hither" (Hollis,
p. 351); and there seems no reason why, since the
Masai song is religious, the Framin song may not be
regarded as religious also.   But we have to remember
that both prayers and spells have a setting of their
own: the desires which they express manifest themselves not only in what is said but in what is done;
and, when we enquire what the Framin women
do whilst they sing the words quoted above, we find
that they dance with brushes in their hands.   The
brushes are quite as essential as the words.   It
is therefore suggested that the whole ceremony is
magical, that the sweeping is sympathetic magic
and the song is a spell.   The words explain what the
action is intended to effect, just as in New Caledonia
when a man has kindled a smoky fire and has
performed certain acts, he "invokes his ancestors
and says, 'Sun! I do this that you may be burning
hot, and eat up all the clouds in the sky'" (Frazer,
ib., 116).   Again, amongst the Masai in time of

drought a charm called ol-kora is thrown into a fire; the old men encircle the fire and sing: —

> "God of the rain-cloud, slake our thirst,
> We know thy far-extending powers,
> As herdsmen lead their kine to drink,
> Refresh us with thy cooling showers."
>   — HOLLIS, p. 348.

If the ol-kora which is thrown into the fire makes it rise in clouds of smoke, resembling the rain-clouds which are desired, then here too the ceremony taken as a whole presents the appearance of a magical rite accompanied by a spoken spell. It is true that in this case the ceremony is reënforced by an appeal to a god, just as in the New Caledonian case it is reënforced by an appeal to ancestor worship. But this may be explained as showing that here we have magic and charms being gradually superseded by religion and prayer; the old formula and the old rite are in process of being suffused by a new spirit, the spirit of religion, which is the very negation and ultimately the destruction of the old spirit of magic.

Before accepting this interpretation, however, which is intended to show the priority of magic to religion, we may notice that it is not the only interpretation of which the facts are susceptible. It is based on the assumption that the words uttered are intended as an explanation of the meaning of the acts performed. If that assumption is correct, then the performer of the ceremony is explaining its meaning and intention to somebody. To whom? In the case of the New Caledonian ceremony, to the ancestral spirits; in the case of the Masai old men, to the god. Thus, the religious aspect of the ceremony appears after all to be an essential part of the ceremony, and not a new element in an old rite. And, then, we may consistently argue that the Framin women who sing, "Our husbands have gone to Ashantee land; may they sweep their enemies off the face of the earth," are either still conscious that they are addressing a prayer to their native god; or that, if they are no longer conscious of the fact, they once were, and what was originally prayer has become by vain repetition a mere spell.

All this is on the assumption that in these ceremonies, the words are intended to explain the meaning of the acts performed, and therefore to explain it to somebody, peradventure he will understand and grant the performer of the ceremony his heart's desire. But, as the consequences of the assumption do not favour the theory that prayer must be preceded by spell, let us discard the assumption that the words explain the meaning of the acts performed. Let us consider the possibility that perhaps the actions which are gone through are meant to explain the words and make them more forcible. It is undeniable that in moments of emotion we express ourselves by gesture and the play of our features as well as by our words; indeed, in reading a play we are apt to miss the full meaning of the words simply because they are not assisted and interpreted by the actor's gestures and features. If we take up this position, that the things done are explanatory of the words uttered and reënforce them, then the sweeping which is acted by the Framin women again is not magical; it simply emphasises the words, "may they sweep their enemies off the face of the earth," and shows to the power appealed to what it is that is desired. The smoke sent up by the New Caledonian ancestor worshipper or the Masai old men is a way of indicating the clouds which they wish to attract or avert respectively. An equally clear case comes from the Kei Islands: "When the warriors have departed, the women return indoors and bring out certain baskets containing fruits and stones. These fruits and stones they anoint and place on a board, murmuring as they do so, 'O lord sun, moon, let the bullets rebound from our husbands, brothers, betrothed, and other relations, just as raindrops rebound from these objects which are smeared with oil'" (Frazer, *op. cit.*, p. 33). It is, I think, perfectly reasonable to regard the act performed as explanatory of the words uttered and of the thing desired; the women themselves explain to their lords, the sun and moon, — with the precision natural to women when explaining what they want, — exactly how they want the bullets to bounce off, just like raindrops. Dr. Frazer, however, from whom I have quoted this illustration, not having perhaps considered the possibility that the acts performed may be explanatory of the words, is compelled to explain the action as magical: "in this custom the ceremony of anointing stones in order that the bullets may recoil from the men like raindrops from the stones is a piece of pure sympathetic or imitative magic." He is therefore compelled to suggest that the prayer to the sun is a prayer that he will give effect to the charm, and is perhaps a later addition. But independently of the possibility that the actions performed are explanatory of the words, or rather that words and actions both are intended to make clear to the sun precisely what the petition is, what tells against Dr. Frazer's suggestion is that the women want the bullets to bounce off, and it is the power of the god to which they appeal and on which they rely for the fulfilment of their prayer.

There is, however, a further consideration which we should perhaps take into account. Man, when he has a desire which he wishes to realise, — and the whole of our life is spent in trying to realise what we wish, — takes all the steps which experience shows to be necessary or reason suggests; and, when he has done everything that he can do, he may still feel that nothing is certain in this life, and the thing may not come off. Under those circumstances he may, and often does, pray that success may attend his efforts. Now Dr. Frazer, in the second edition of his *Golden Bough*, wishing to show that the period of religion was preceded by a non-religious period in the history of mankind, suggests that at first man had no idea that his attempts to realise his desires could fail, and that it was his "tardy recognition" of the fact that led him to religion. This tardy recognition, he says, probably "proceeded very slowly, and required long ages for its more or less perfect accomplishment. For the recognition of man's powerlessness to influence the course of

nature on a grand scale must have been gradual"
(I, 78). I would suggest, however, that it cannot
have taken "long ages" for savage man to discover
that his wishes and his plans did not always come
off. It is, I think, going too far to imagine that
for long ages man had no idea that his attempts to
realise his desires could fail. If religion arises, as
Dr. Frazer suggests, when man recognises his own
weakness and his own powerlessness, often, to effect
what he most desires, then man in his most primitive and most helpless condition must have been
most ready to recognise that there were powers
other than himself, and to desire, that is to pray
for, their assistance. Doubtless it would be at the
greater crises, times of pestilence, drought, famine
and war, that his prayers would be most insistent;
but it is in the period of savagery that famine is most
frequent and drought most to be feared. Against
them he takes all the measures known to him, all
the practical steps which natural science, as understood by him, can suggest. Now his theory and
practice include many things which, though they are
in later days regarded as uncanny and magical, are
to him the ordinary natural means of producing the
effects which he desires. But when he has taken all

the steps which practical reason suggests, and experience of the past approves, savage man, harassed
by the dread of approaching drought or famine, may
still breathe out the Manganja prayer, "Hear thou,
O God, and send rain." When, however, he does
so, it is, I suggest, doubly erroneous to infer that
this prayer takes the place of a spell or that apart
from the prayer the acts performed are, and originally were, magical. These acts may be based on the
principle that like produces like and may be performed
as the ordinary, natural means for producing the effect,
which have nothing magical about them. And they are
accompanied by a prayer which is not a mere explanation or statement of the purpose with which the acts are
performed, but is the expression of the heart's desire.

No à priori proofs of any cogency, therefore, have
been adduced by Dr. Frazer, and none therefore are
likely to be produced by any one else, to show that
there was ever a period in the history of man when
prayers and religion were unknown to him. The
question remains whether any actual instances are
known to the science of religion. Unfortunately, as
I pointed out at the beginning of this lecture, so
neglected by the science of religion has been the
subject of prayer that even now we are scarcely

able to go beyond the statement made more than a quarter of a century ago by Professor Tylor that, "at low levels of civilisation there are many races who distinctly admit the existence of spirits, but are not certainly known to pray to them even in thought" (*P. C.* II, 364). Professor Tylor's statement is properly guarded: there are races not certainly known to pray. The possibility that they may yet be discovered to make prayers is not excluded.

Now, if we turn to one of the lowest levels of culture, that of the Australian black fellows, we shall find that there is much doubt amongst students whether the "aborigines have consciously any form of religion whatever" (Howitt, *Native Tribes of S. E. Australia*), and in southeast Australia Mr. Howitt thinks it cannot be alleged that they have, though their beliefs are such that they might easily have developed into an actual religion (p. 507). Now one of the tribes of southeast Australia is that of the Dieri. With them rain is very important, for periods of drought are frequent; and "rain-making ceremonies are considered of much consequence" (p. 394). The ceremonies are symbolic: there is "blood to symbolise the rain" and two large stones "representing gathering

M

clouds presaging rain," just as the New Caledonian sends up clouds of smoke to symbolise rain-clouds, and the Masai, we have conjectured, throw ol-kora into the fire for the same purpose. But the New Caledonian not only performs the actions prescribed for the rite, he also invokes the spirits of his ancestors; and the Masai not only go through the proper dance, but call upon the god of the rain-cloud. The Dieri, however, ought to be content with their symbolic or sympathetic magic and not offer up any prayer. But, being unaware of this fact, they do pray: they call "upon the rain-making *Muramuras* to give them power to make a heavy rainfall, crying out in loud voices the impoverished state of the country, and the half-starved condition of the tribe, in consequence of the difficulty in procuring food in sufficient quantity to preserve life" (p. 394). The *Mura-muras* seem to be ancestral spirits, like those invoked by the New Caledonian. If we turn to the Euahlayi tribe of northwestern New South Wales, we find that at the Boorah rites a prayer is offered to Byamee, "asking him to let the blacks live long, for they have been faithful to his charge as shown by the observance of the Boorah ceremony" (L. Parker, *The Euahlayi*

Tribe, p. 79). That is the prayer of the community to Byamee, and is in conformity with what we have noted before, viz. that it is with the desires of the community that the god of the community is concerned. Another prayer, the nature of which is not stated by Mrs. Parker, by whom the information is given us, is put up at funerals, presumably to Byamee by the community or its representative. Mrs. Parker adds: "Though we say that actually these people have but two attempts at prayers, one at the grave and one at the inner Boorah ring, I think perhaps we are wrong. When a man invokes aid on the eve of battle, or in his hour of danger and need; when a woman croons over her baby an incantation to keep him honest and true, and that he shall be spared in danger, — surely these croonings are of the nature of prayers born of the same elementary frame of mind as our more elaborate litanies." As an instance of the croonings Mrs. Parker gives the mother's song over her baby, as soon as it begins to crawl: —

> "Kind be,
>   Do not steal,
>   Do not touch what to another belongs,
>   Leave all such alone,
>   Kind be."

These instances may suffice to show that it would not have been safe to infer, a year or two ago, from the fact that the Australians were not known to pray, that therefore prayer was unknown to them. Indeed, we may safely go farther and surmise that other instances besides those noted really exist, though they have not been observed or if observed have not been understood. Among the northern tribes of central Australia rites are performed to secure food, just as they are performed by the Dieri to avert drought. The Dieri rites are accompanied by a prayer, as we have seen. The Kaitish rites to promote the growth of grass are accompanied by the singing of words, which "have no meaning known to the natives of the present day" (Spencer and Gillen, *Northern Tribes*, p. 292). Amongst the Mara tribe the rain-making rite consists simply in "singing" the water, drinking it and spitting it out in all directions. In the Anula tribe "dugongs are a favourite article of food," and if the natives desire to bring them out from the rocks, they "can do so by 'singing' and throwing sticks at the rocks" (*ib.*, pp. 313, 314). It is reasonable to suppose that in all these cases the "singing" is now merely a charm. But if we remember that prayers, when their meaning is forgotten, pass by vain repetitions into mere charms, we may also reasonably suppose that these Australian charms are degraded prayers; and we shall be confirmed in this supposition to some extent by the fact that in the Kaitish tribes the words sung "have no meaning known to the natives of the present day." If the meaning has evaporated, the religion may have evaporated with it. That the rites, of which the "singing" is an essential part, have now become magical and are used and understood to be practised purely to promote the supply of dugongs and other articles of food, may be freely admitted; but it is unsafe to infer that the purpose with which the rites continue to be practised is the whole of the purpose with which they were originally performed. If the meaning of the "singing" has passed entirely away, the meaning of the rites may have suffered a change. At the present day the rite is understood to increase the supply of dugongs or other articles of food. But it may have been used originally for other purposes. Presumably rites of a similar kind, certainly of some kind, are practised by the Australians who have for their totem the blow-fly, the water-beetle, or the evening star. But they do not eat flies or beetles. Their original purpose in choosing the evening star cannot have been to increase its number. Nor can that have been the object of choosing the mosquito for a totem. But if the object of the rites is not to increase the number of mosquitoes, flies, and beetles, it need not in the first instance have been the object with which the rites were celebrated in the case of other totems.

Let us now return to Professor Tylor's statement that "at low levels of civilisation there are many races who distinctly admit the existence of spirits, but are not certainly known to pray to them even in thought." The number of those races who are not known to pray is being reduced, as we have seen. And I think we may go even farther than that and say that where the existence of spirits is not merely believed in, but is utilised for the purpose of establishing permanent relations between a community and a spirit, we may safely infer that the community offers prayer to the spirit, even though the fact may have escaped the notice of travellers. The reason why we may infer it is that at the lower levels of civilisation we meet with religion, in Höffding's words, "in the guise of desire." We may put the same truth in other words and say that religion is from the beginning practical. Such prayers as are known to us to be put up by the lowest races are always practical: they may be definite petitions for definite goods such as harvest or rain or victory in time of war; or they may be general petitions such as that of the Khonds: "We are ignorant of what it is good for us to ask for. You know what is good for us. Give it us." But in any case what the god of a community is there for is to promote the good of the community. It is because the savage has petitions to put up that he believes there are powers who can grant his petitions. Prayer is the very root of religion. When the savage has taken every measure he knows of to produce the result he desires, he then goes on to pray for the rainfall he desires, crying out in a loud voice "the impoverished state of the country and the half-starved condition of the tribe." It is true that it is in moments of stress particularly, if not solely, that the savage turns to his god — and the same may be said of many of us — but it is with confidence and hope that he turns to him. If he had no confidence and no hope, he would offer no prayers. But he has hope, he has faith; and every time he prays his heart says, if his words do not, "in Thee, Lord, do we put our trust."

That prayer is the essence, the very breath, of religion, without which it dies, is shown by the fact that amongst the very lowest races of mankind we find frequent traditions of the existence of a high god or supreme being, the creator of the world and the father of mankind. The numerous traces of this dying tradition have been collected by the untiring energy and the unrivalled knowledge of Mr. Andrew Lang in his book, *The Making of Religion*. In West Africa Dr. Nassau (*Fetichism in West Africa*, pp. 36 ff.) "hundreds of times" (p. 37) has found that "they know of a Being superior to themselves, of whom they themselves," he says, "inform me that he is the Maker and the Father." What is characteristic of the belief of the savages in this god is that, in Dr. Nassau's words, "it is an accepted belief, but it does not often influence their life. 'God is not in all their thought.' In practice they give Him no worship." The belief is in fact a dying tradition; and it is dying because prayer is not offered to this remote and traditional god. I say that the belief is a dying tradition, and I say so because its elements, which are all found present and active where a community believes in, prays to, and worships the god of the community, are found partially, but only partially, present where the belief survives but as a tradition. Thus, for instance, where the belief is fully operative, the god of the community sanctions the morality of the community; but sometimes where the belief has become merely traditional, this traditional god is supposed to take no interest in the community and exercises no ethical influence over the community. Thus, in West Africa, Nyankupon is "ignored rather than worshipped." In the Andaman Islands, on the other hand, where the god Puluga is still angered by sin or wrong-doing, he is pitiful to those in pain or distress and "sometimes deigns to afford relief" (Lang p, 212 quoting *Man, J. A. I.*, XII, 158). Again, where the belief in the god of the community is fully operative, the occasions on which the prayers of the community are offered are also the occasions on which sacrifice is made. Where sacrifice and prayers are not offered, the belief may still for a time survive, at is does among the Fuegians. They make no sacrifice and, as far as is known, offer no prayers; but to kill a man brings down the wrath of their god, the big man in the woods: "Rain come down, snow come down, hail come down, wind blow, blow, very much blow.

Very bad to kill man. Big man in woods no like it, he very angry" (Lang, p. 188, quoting Fitzroy, II, 180). But when sacrifice and prayer cease, the ultimate outcome is that which is found amongst the West African natives, who, as Dr. Nassau tells us (p. 38), say with regard to Anzam, whom they admit to be their Creator and Father, "Why should we care for him? He does not help nor harm us. It is the spirits who can harm us whom we fear and worship, and for whom we care." Who the spirits are Dr. Nassau does not say, but they must be either the other gods of the place or the fetich spirits. And the reason why Anzam is no longer believed to help or harm the natives is obviously that, from some cause or other, there is now no longer any established form of worship of him. The community of which he was originally the god may have broken up, or more probably may have been broken up, with the result that the congregation which met to offer prayer and sacrifice to Anzam was scattered; and the memory of him alone survives. Nothing would be more natural, then, than that the natives, when asked by Dr. Nassau, "Why do you not worship him?" (p. 38), should invent a reason, viz. that it is no use worshipping

him now — the truth being that the form of worship has perished for reasons now no longer present
to the natives' mind. In any case, when prayers
cease to be offered — whether because the community is broken up or because some new quarter
is discovered to which prayers can be offered with
greater hope of success — when prayers, for any
reason, do cease to be offered to a god, the worship
of him begins to cease also, for the breath of life
has departed from it.

In this lecture, as my subject is primitive religion,
I have made no attempt to trace the history of
prayer farther than the highest point which it reaches
in the lower levels of religion. That is the point
reached by the Khond prayer: "We are ignorant
of what it is good to ask for. You know what is
good for us. Give it us." That is also the highest
point reached by the most religious mind amongst
the ancient Greeks: Socrates prayed the gods simply
for things good, because the gods knew best what
is good (Xen., *Mem.*, I, iii, 2). The general impres-
sion left on one's mind by the prayers offered in
this stage of religious development is that man is
here and the gods are — there. But "there" is
such a long way off. And yet, far off as it is, man

never came to think it was so far off that the gods could not hear. The possibility of man's entering into some sort of communication with them was always present. Nay! more, a community of interests between him and them was postulated: the gods were to promote the interests of the community, and man was to serve the gods. On occasions when sacrifice was made and prayer was offered, the worshippers entered into the presence of God, and communion with Him was sought; but stress was laid rather on the sacrifice offered than on the prayers sent up. The communion at which animal sacrifice aimed may have been gross at times, and at others mystic; but it was the sacrifice rather than the prayer which accompanied it that was regarded as essential to the communion desired, as the means of bridging the gap between man here and the gods there. If, however, the gap was to be bridged, a new revelation was necessary, one revealing the real nature of the sacrifice required by God, and of the communion desired by man. And that revelation is made in Our Lord's Prayer. With the most earnest and unfeigned desire to use the theory of evolution as a means of ordering the facts of the history of religion and of enabling us —

so far as it can enable us — to understand them, one is bound to notice as a fact that the theory of evolution is unable to account for or explain the revelation, made in Our Lord's Prayer, of the spirit which is both human and divine. It is the beam of light which, when turned on the darkness of the past, enables us to see whither man with his prayers and his sacrifices had been blindly striving, the place where he fain would be. It is the surest beacon the missionary can hold out to those who are still in darkness and who show by the fact that they pray — if only for rain, for harvest, and victory over all their enemies — that they are battling with the darkness and that they have not turned entirely away from the light of His countenance who is never at any time far from any one of us. Their heart within them is ready to bear witness. Religion is present in them, if only under "the guise of desire"; but it is "the desire of all nations" for which they yearn.

There are, Höffding says, "two tendencies in the nature of religious feeling: on the one hand there is the need to collect and concentrate ourselves, to resign ourselves, to feel ourselves supported and carried by a power raised above all struggle and opposition and beyond all change. But within the religious consciousness another need makes itself felt, the need of feeling that in the midst of the struggle we have a fellow-struggler at our side, a fellow-struggler who knows from his own experience what it is to suffer and meet resistance" (*The Philosophy of Religion*, § 54). Between these two tendencies Höffding discovers an opposition or contradiction, an "antinomy of religious feeling." But it is precisely because Christianity alone of all religions recognises both needs that it transcends the antinomy. The antinomy is indeed purely intellectual. Höffding himself says, "only when recollection, collation, and comparison are possible do we discover the opposition or the contradiction between the two tendencies." And in saying that, inasmuch as recollection, collation, and comparison are intellectual processes, he admits that the antinomy is intellectual. That it is not an antinomy of religious feeling is shown by the fact that the two needs exist, that is to say, are both felt. To say *à priori* that both cannot be satisfied is useless in face of the fact that those who feel them find that Christianity satisfies them.

SACRIFICE

In my last lecture I called attention to the fact that the subject of prayer has been strangely neglected by the science of religion. Religion, in whatever form it manifests itself, is essentially practical; man desires to enter into communication or into communion with his god, and in so doing he has a practical purpose in view. That purpose may be to secure a material blessing of a particular kind, such as victory in war or the enjoyment of the fruits of the earth in their due season, or the purpose may be to offer thanks for a harvest and to pray for a continuance of prosperity generally. Or the purpose of prayer may be to ask for deliverance from material evils, such as famine or plague. Or it may be to ask for deliverance from moral evils and for power to do God's will. In a word, if man had no prayer to make, the most powerful, if not the only, motive inciting him to seek communion would be wanting. Now, to some of us it may seem à priori that there is no reason why the communion thus sought in prayer should require any external rite to sanction or condition it. If that is our *à priori* view, we shall be the more surprised to find that in actual fact an external rite has always been felt to be essential; and that rite has always been and still is sacrifice, in one or other of its forms. Or, to put the same fact in another way, public worship has been from the beginning the condition without which private worship could not begin and without which private worship cannot continue. To any form of religion, whatever it be, it is essential, if it is to be religion, that there shall be a community of worshippers and a god worshipped. The bond which unites the worshippers with one another and with their god is religion. From the beginning the public worship in which the worshippers have united has expressed itself in rites — rites of sacrifice — and in the prayers of the community. To the end, the prayers offered are prayers to "Our Father"; and if the worshipper is spatially separated from, he is spiritually united to, his fellow-worshippers even in private prayer.

We may then recognise that prayer logically and ultimately implies sacrifice in one or other of its senses; and that sacrifice as a rite is meaningless and impossible without prayer. But if we recognise that sacrifice wherever it occurs implies prayer, then the fact that the observers of savage or barbarous rites have described the ritual acts of sacrifice, but have not observed or have neglected to report the prayers implied, will not lead us into the error of imagining that sacrifice is a rite which can exist — that it can have a religious existence — without prayer. We may attend to either, the sacrifice or to the prayer, as we may attend either to the concavity or the convexity of a curve, but we may not deny the existence and presence of the one because our attention happens to be concentrated on the other. The relation in primitive religion of the one to the other we may express by saying that prayer states the motive with which the sacrifice is made, and that sacrifice is essential to the prayer, which would not be efficacious without the sacrifice. The reason why a community can address the god which it worships is that the god is felt to be identified in some way with the community and to have its interests in his charge and care. And the rite of sacrifice is felt to make the identification more real. Prayer, again, is possible only to the god to whom the community is known; with whom it is identified, more or less; and with whom, when his help is required, the com-

munity seeks to identify itself more effectually.
The means of that identification without which the
prayers of the community would be ineffectual is
sacrifice. The earliest form of sacrifice may probably be taken to be the sacrifice of an animal, followed by a sacrificial meal. Later, when the god
has a stated place in which he is believed to manifest
himself, — tree or temple, — then the identification
may be effected by attaching offerings to the tree
or temple. But in either case what is sought by the
offering dedicated or the meal of sacrifice is in a
word "incorporation." The worshippers desire to
feel that they are at one with the spirit whom they
worship. And the desire to experience this sense of
union is particularly strong when plague or famine
makes it evident that some estrangement has taken
place between the god and the community which is
normally in his care and under his protection. The
sacrifices and prayers that are offered in such a case
obviously do not open up communication for the first
time between the god and his tribe: they revive and
reënforce a communion which is felt to exist already,
even though temporal misfortunes, such as drought
or famine, testify that it has been allowed by the
tribe to become less close than it ought to be, or that

it has been strained by transgressions on the part of individual members of the community. But it is not only in times of public distress that the community approaches its god with sacrifice and prayer. It so happens that the prayers offered for victory in war or for rain or for deliverance from famine are instances of prayer of so marked a character that they have forced themselves on the notice of travellers in all parts of the world, from the Eskimo to the Australian black fellows or the negroes of Africa. And it was to this class of prayers that I called your attention principally in the last lecture. But they are, when we come to think of it, essentially occasional prayers, prayers that are offered at the great crises of tribal life, when the very existence of the tribe is at stake. Such crises, however, by their very nature are not regular or normal; and it would be an error to suppose that it is only on these occasions that prayers are made by savage or barbarous peoples. If we wish to discover the earliest form of regularly recurring public worship, we must look for some regularly recurring occasion for it. One such regularly recurring occasion is harvest time, another is seed time, another is the annual ceremonial at which the boys who attain in the course of the year to the age of manhood are initiated into the secrets or "mysteries" of the tribe. These are the chief and perhaps the only regularly recurring occasions of public worship as distinguished from the irregular crises of war, pestilence, drought, and famine which affect the community as a whole, and from the irregular occasions when the individual member of the community prays for offspring or for delivery from sickness or for success in the private undertaking in which he happens to be engaged.

Of the regularly recurring occasions of public worship I will select, to begin with, the rites which are associated with harvest time. And I will do so partly because the science of religion provides us with very definite particulars both as to the sacrifices and as to the prayers which are usually made on these occasions; and partly because the prayers that are made are of a special kind and throw a fresh light on the nature of the communion that the tribe seeks to effect by means of the sacrificial offering.

At Saa, in the Solomon Islands, yams are offered, and the person offering them cries in a loud voice, "This is yours to eat" (Frazer, *G. B.*[2], II, 465). In

the Society Islands the formula is, "Here, Tari, I have
brought you something to eat" (*ib.*, 469). In Indo-
China, the invitation is the same: "Taste, O goddess, these first-fruits which have just been reaped"
(*ib.*, 325). There are no actually expressed words
of thanks in these instances; but we may safely
conjecture that the offerings are thank-offerings and
that the feeling with which the offerings are made is
one of gratitude and thankfulness. Thus in Ceram
we are told that first-fruits are offered "as a token of
gratitude" (*ib.*, 463). On the Niger the Onitsha
formula is explicit: "I thank God for being permitted to eat the new yam" (*ib.*, 325). At Tjumba
in the East Indies, "vessels filled with rice are presented as a thank-offering to the gods" (*ib.*, 462).
The people of Nias on these occasions offer thanks
for the blessings bestowed on them (*ib.*, 463). By a
very natural transition of thought and feeling, thankfulness for past favours leads to prayer for the continuance of favour in the future. Thus in Tana, in
the New Hebrides, the formula is: "Compassion-
ate father! here is some food for you; eat it; be
kind to us on account of it" (*ib.*, 464); while the
Basutos say: "Thank you, gods; give us bread
to-morrow also" (*ib.*, 459); and in Tonga the prayers

made at the offering of first-fruits implore the protection of the gods, and beseech them for welfare
generally, though in especial for the fruits of the
earth (*ib.*, 466).

The prayers of primitive man which I quoted in
my last lecture were in the nature of petitions or
requests, as was natural and indeed inevitable in
view of the fact that they were preferred on occasions
when the tribe was in exceptional distress and required the aid of the gods on whose protection the
community relied.   But the prayers which I have
just quoted are not in their essence petitions or
requests, even though in some cases they tend to
become so.   They are essentially prayers of thanksgiving and the offerings made are thank-offerings.
Thus our conception of primitive prayer must be
extended to include both mental attitudes — that
of thankfulness for past or present blessings as well
as the hope of blessings yet to come.   And inasmuch
as sacrifice is the concomitant of prayer, we must
recognise that sacrificial offerings also serve as the
expression of both mental attitudes.   And we must
note that in the regularly recurring form of public
or tribal worship with which we are now dealing
the dominant feeling to which expression is given is

that of thankfulness. The tribe seeks for communion with its god for the purpose of expressing its thanks. Even the savage who simply says, "Here, Tari, I have brought you something to eat," or, still more curtly, "This is yours to eat," is expressing thanks, albeit in savage fashion. And the means which the savage adopts for securing that communion which he seeks to renew regularly with the tribal god is a sacrificial meal, of which the god and his worshippers partake. Throughout the whole ceremony, whether we regard the spoken words or the acts performed, there is no suggestion of magic and no possibility of twisting the ceremony into a piece of magic intended to produce some desired result or to exercise any constraint over the powers to which the ceremony is addressed. The mental attitude is that of thankfulness.

Now, it is, I venture to suggest, impossible to dissociate from the first-fruits ceremonials which I have described the ceremonies observed by Australian black fellows on similar occasions. And it is also impossible to overlook the differences between the ceremony in Australia and the ceremony elsewhere. In Australia, as elsewhere, when the time of year arrives at which the food becomes fit for eating, a ceremony has to be performed before custom permits the food to be eaten freely. In Australia, as elsewhere, a ceremonial eating, a sacramental meal, has to take place. But whereas elsewhere the god of the community is expressly invited to partake of the sacramental meal, even though he be not mentioned by name and though the invitation take the curt form of "This is yours to eat," in Australia no words whatever are spoken; the person who performs the ceremony performs it indeed with every indication of reverential feeling, he eats solemnly and sparingly, that is to say formally and because the eating is a matter of ritual, but no reference is made by him so far as we know, to any god. How then are we to explain the absence of any such reference? There seems to me to be only one explanation which is reasonably possible. It is that in the Australian ceremony, which would be perfectly intelligible and perfectly in line with the ceremony as it occurs everywhere else, the reference to the god who is or was invited to partake of the first-fruits has in the process of time and, we must add, in the course of religious decay, gradually dropped out. The invitation may never have been more ample than the curt form, "This is yours to eat." Even in the absence of any verbal invitation whatever, a gesture may long have sufficed to indicate what was in the mind and was implied by the act of the savage performing the ceremony. Words may not have been felt necessary to explain what every person present at the ceremony knew to be the purpose of the rite. But in the absence of any verbal formula whatever the purpose and meaning of the rite would be apt to pass out of mind, to evaporate, even though custom maintained, as it does in Australia to this day maintain, the punctual and punctilious performance of the outward ceremony. I suggest, therefore, that in Australia, as elsewhere, the solemn eating of the first-fruits has been a sacramental meal of which both the god and his worshippers were partakers. The alternative is to my mind much less probable: it is to use the Australian ceremony as it now exists to explain the origin of the ceremony as we find it elsewhere. In Australia it is not now apparently associated with the worship of any god; therefore it may be argued in other countries also it was not originally part of the worship of any god either. If, then, it was not an act of public worship originally, how are we to understand it? The suggestion is that the fruits of the earth or the animals which become the food of man are, until they become fit for eating, regarded as sacred or taboo, and therefore may not be eaten. That suggestion derives some support from the fact that in Australia anything that is eaten may be a totem and being a totem is taboo. But if it is thus sacred, then in order to be eaten it must be "desacralised," the taboo must be taken off. And it is suggested that that precisely is what is effected by the ceremonial eating of the totem by the headman of the totem clan: the totem is desacralised by the mere fact that it is formally and ceremonially eaten by the headman, after which it may be consumed by others as an ordinary article of food. But this explanation of the first-fruits ceremony is based upon an assumption which is contrary to the facts of the case as it occurs in Australia. It assumes that the plant or the animal until desacralised is taboo to all members of the tribe, and that none of them can eat it until it has been desacralised by the ceremonial eating. But the assumption is false; the plant or animal is sacred and taboo only to members of the clan whose totem, it is. It is not sacred to the vast majority of the tribe, for they have totems of their own; to them it is not sacred or taboo, they may kill it — and they do — without breaking any taboo. The ceremonial eating of the first-fruits raises no taboo as far as the tribe generally is concerned, for the plant or animal is not taboo to them. As far as the tribe generally is concerned, no process of desacralisation takes place and none is effected by the ceremonial eating. It is the particular totem group alone which is affected by the ceremony; and the inference which it seems to me preferable to draw is that the ceremonial eating of the first-fruits is, or rather has been, in Australia what it is elsewhere, viz. an instance of prayer and sacrifice in which the worshippers of a god are brought into periodic — in this case annual — communion with their god. The difference between the Australian case and others seems to be that in the other cases the god who partakes of the first-fruits is the god of the whole community, while in Australia he is the god of the particular totem group and is analogous to the family gods who are worshipped elsewhere, even where there is a tribal or national god to be worshipped as well.

We are then inclined, for these and other reasons, to explain the ceremonial eating of the totem plant or animal in Australia by the analogy of the ceremonial eating of first-fruits elsewhere, and to regard the ceremony as being in all cases an act of worship, in which at harvest time the worshippers of a god seek communion with him by means of sacrifice and prayers of thanksgiving. But if we take this view of the sacrifice and prayers offered at harvest time, we shall be inclined to regard the rites which are performed at seed time, or the period analogous to it, as being also possibly, in part, of a religious character. In the case of agricultural peoples it is beyond doubt that some of the ceremonies are religious in character: where the food plant is itself regarded as a deity or the mode in which a deity is manifested, not only may there be at harvest time a sacramental meal in which, as amongst the Aztecs, the deity is formally "communicated" to his worshippers, but at seed time sacrifice and prayer may be made to the deity. Such a religious ceremony, whatever be the degree of civilisation or semicivilisation which has been reached by those who observe the ceremony, does not of course take the place of the agricultural operations which are necessary if the fruits are to be produced in due season. And the combination of the religious rites and the agricultural operations does not convert the agricultural operations into magical operations, or prove that the religious rites are merely pieces of magic intended to constrain the superior power of the deity concerned. Indeed, if among the operations performed at seed time we find some that from the point of view of modern science are perfectly ineffectual, as vain as eating tiger to make you bold, we shall be justified in regarding them as pieces of primitive science, eventually discarded indeed in the progress of advancing knowledge, but originally practised (on the principle that like produces like) as the natural means of producing the effect desired. If we so regard them, we shall escape the error of considering them to be magical; and we shall have no difficulty in distinguishing them from the religious rites which may be combined with them. Further, where harvest time is marked by the offering of sacrifice and prayers of thanksgiving, we may not unreasonably take it that the religious rites observed at seed time or the period analogous to it are in the nature of sacrifice and prayers addressed to the appropriate deity to beseech him to favour the growth of the plant or animal in question. In a word, the practice of giving thanks to a god at harvest time for the harvest creates a reasonable presumption that prayer is offered to him at seed time; and if thanks are given at a period analogous to harvest time by a people like the Australian black fellows, who have no domesticated plants or animals, prayers of the nature of petitions may be offered by them at the period analogous to seed time.

The deity to whom prayers are offered at the one period and thanksgiving is made at the other may be, as in the case of the Aztec Xilonen, or the Hindoo Maize-mother, the spirit of the plant envisaged as a deity; or may be, not a "departmental" deity of this kind, but a supreme deity having power over all things.   But when we turn from the regularly recurring acts of public worship connected with seed time and harvest to the regularly recurring ceremonies at which the boys of a tribe are initiated into the duties and rights of manhood, it is obvious that the deity concerned in them, even if we assume (as is by no means necessary) that he was originally "departmental" and at first connected merely with the growth of a plant or animal, must be regarded at the initiation ceremonies as a god having in his care all the interests of that tribe of which the boys to be initiated are about to become full members.   Unmistakable traces of such a deity are found amongst the Australian black fellows in the "father of all," "the all-father" described by Mr. Howitt.   The

worship of the "all-father" is indeed now of a frag
mentary kind; but it fortunately happens that in
the case of one tribe, the Euahlayi, we have evidence,
rescued by Mrs. Langloh Parker, to show that prayer
is offered to Byamee; the Euahlayi pray to him for
long life, because they have kept his law. The
nature of Byamee's law may safely be inferred from
the fact that at this festival, both amongst the Euahlayi and other Australians, the boys who are
being initiated are taught the moral laws or the
customary morality of the tribe. But though prayers are still offered by the Euahlayi and may have
at one time been offered by all the Australian tribes,
there is no evidence at present to show that the prayer
is accompanied by a sacrifice, as is customary amongst
tribes whose worship has not disintegrated so much
as is the case amongst the Australians.

The ceremonies by which boys are admitted to
the status of manhood are, probably amongst all
the peoples of the earth who observe them, of a
religious character, for the simple reason that the
community to which the boy is admitted when he
attains the age of manhood is a community, united
together by religious bonds as a community worshipping the same god or gods; and it is to the wor-

ship and the service of these gods that he is admitted. But the ceremonies themselves vary too much to allow of our drawing from them any valuable or important conclusion as to the nature and import of sacrifice as a religious institution. On the other hand, the ceremonies observed at harvest time, or the analogous period, have, wherever they occur, such marked similarity among themselves, and the institution of prayer and sacrifice is such a prominent feature in them, that the evidence they afford must be decisive for us in attempting to form a theory of sacrifice. Nor can we dissociate the ceremonies observed in spring from the harvest ceremonies; as Dr. Frazer remarks (*G. B.*, II, 190), "Plainly these spring and harvest customs are based on the same ancient modes of thought and form parts of the same primitive heathendom." What, then, are these "ancient modes of thought" and what the primitive customs based upon them? We may, I think, classify them in four groups. If we are to take first those instances in which the "ancient mode of thought" is most clearly expressed — whether because they are the most fully developed or because they retain the ancient mode most faithfully and with the least disintegration — we must

turn to ancient Mexico and Peru. In Mexico
a paste idol or dough image of the god was made;
the priest hurled a dart into its breast; and this was
called the killing of the god, "so that his body might
be eaten." The dough image was broken and the
pieces were given in the manner of a communion to
the people, "who received it with such tears, fear,
and reverence, as it was an admirable thing," says
Father Acosta, "saying that they did eat the flesh
and bones of God." Or, again, an image of the
goddess Chicomecoatl was made of dough and exhibited by the priest, saying, "This is your god."
All kinds of maize, beans, etc., were offered to it and
then were eaten in the temple "in a general scram-
ble, take who could." In Peru ears of maize were
dressed in rich garments and worshipped as the
Mother of the Maize; or little loaves of maize mingled
with the blood of sheep were made; the priest gave
to each of the people a morsel of these loaves, " and
all did receive and eat these pieces," and prayed that
the god "would show them favour, granting them
children and happy years and abundance and all
that they required." In this, the first group of
instances, it is plain beyond all possibility of gain-
saying that the spring and harvest customs consist

o

of the worship of a god, of sacrifice and prayers to him, and of a communion which bound the worshippers to one another and to him.

Our second group of instances consists of cases in which the corn or dough or paste is not indeed made into the form or image of a god, but, as Dr. Frazer says (*G. B.* II, 318), "the new corn is itself eaten sacramentally, that is, as the body of the corn spirit." The spirit thus worshipped may not yet have acquired a proper name; the only designation used may have been such a one as the Hindoo Bhogaldái, meaning simply Cotton-mother. Indeed, even amongst the Peruvians, the goddess had not yet acquired a proper name, but was known only as the Mother of the Maize. But precisely because the stage illustrated in our second group of instances is not so highly developed as in Mexico or Peru it is much more widely spread. It is found in the East Indian island of Buro, amongst the Alfoors of Minahassa, in the Celebes, in the Neilgherry Hills of South India, in the Hindoo Koosh, in Indo-China, on the Niger, amongst the Zulus and the Pondos, and amongst the Creek, Seminole, and Natchez Indians (*ib.* 321–342). In this, the second group of instances, then, though the god may have no special, proper, name, and though no image of him is made out of the dough or paste, still "the new corn is itself eaten sacramentally, that is as the body of the corn spirit"; by means of the sacramental eating, of sacrifice and prayer, communion between the god and his worshippers is renewed and maintained.

The third group of instances consists of the harvest customs of northern Europe — the harvest supper and the rites of the Corn-mother or the Corn-maiden or the Kern Baby. It can scarcely be contended that these rites and customs, so far as they survive at the present day, retain, if they ever had, any religious value; they are performed as a matter of tradition and custom and not because any one knows why they are performed. But that they originally had a meaning — even though now it has evaporated — cannot be doubted. Nor can it be doubted that the meaning, if it is to be recovered, must be recovered by means of the comparative method. And, if the comparative method is to be applied, the Corn-mother of northern Europe cannot be dissociated from the Maize-mother of ancient Peru. But if we go thus far, then we must, with Dr. Frazer (*ib.* 288), recognise "clearly the sacramental character of the harvest-supper," in which, "as a substitute for the real flesh of the divine being, bread and dumplings are made and eaten sacramentally." Thus, once more, harvest customs testify in northern Europe, as elsewhere, to the fact that there was once a stated, annual, period at which communion between the god and his worshipper was sought by prayer and sacrifice.

The North-European harvest customs are further interesting and important because, if they are clearly connected on the one hand with the groups of instances already given, they are also connected on the other with the group to which we have yet to call attention. Thus far the wheat or maize, if not eaten in the form of little loaves or cakes, has been made into a dough image, or else the ears of maize have been dressed in rich garments to indicate that they represent the Mother of the Maize; and in Europe also both forms of symbolism are found. But in northern Europe, the corn spirit is also believed to be manifested, Dr. Frazer says, in "the animal which is present in the corn and is caught or killed in the last sheaf." The animal may be a wolf, dog, cock, hare, cat, goat, bull, cow, horse, or pig. "The animal is slain and its flesh and blood are partaken of by the harvesters," and, Dr. Frazer says, "these customs bring out clearly the sacramental character of the harvest supper." Now, this manifestation of the corn spirit in animal form is not confined to Europe; it occurs for instance in Guinea and in all the provinces and districts of China. And it is important as forming a link between the agricultural and the pre-agricultural periods; in Dr. Frazer's words, "hunting and pastoral tribes, as well as agricultural peoples, have been in the habit of killing their gods" (*ib.* 366). In the pastoral period, as well as in agricultural times, the god who is worshipped by the tribe and with whom the tribe seeks communion by means of prayer and sacrifice, may manifest himself in animal form, and "the animal is slain and its flesh and blood are partaken of."

We now come to the fourth and the last of our groups of instances. It consists of the rites observed by Australian tribes. Amongst these tribes too there is what Dr. Frazer terms "a sacramental eating" of the totem plant or animal. Thus Central Australian black men of the kangaroo totem eat a little kangaroo flesh, as a sacrament (Spencer and Gillen, p. 204 ff.). Now, it is impossible, I think, to dissociate the Australian rite, to separate this fourth group, from the three groups already described. In Australia, as in the other cases, the customs are observed in spring and harvest time, and in harvest time, in Australia as well as elsewhere, there is a solemn and sparing eating of the plant or animal; and, in Dr. Frazer's words, "plainly these spring and harvest customs are based on the same ancient modes of thought, and form part of the same primitive heathendom." What, then, is this ancient and primitive mode of thought? In all the cases except the Australian, the thought manifestly implied and expressed is that by the solemn eating of the plant or the animal, or the dough image or paste idol, or the little loaves, the community enters into communion with its god, or renews communion with him. On this occasion the Peruvians prayed for children, happy years and abundance. On this occasion, even among the Australians, the Euahlayi tribe pray for long life, because they have kept Byamee's law. It would not, therefore, be unreasonable to interpret the Australian custom by the same ancient mode of thought which explains the custom wherever else — and that is all over the world — it is found. But perhaps, if we can find some other interpretation

of the Australian custom, we should do better to
reverse the process and explain the spring and harvest customs which are found elsewhere by means of,
and in accordance with, the Australian custom.
Now another interpretation of the Australian custom
has been put forward by Dr. Frazer. He treats the
Australian ceremony as being a piece of pure magic,
the purpose of which is to promote the growth and
increase of the plants and animals which provide
the black fellows with food. But if we start from
this point of view, we must go further and say that
amongst other peoples than the Australian the killing of the representative animal of the spirit of
vegetation is, in Dr. Frazer's words, "a magical rite
intended to assure the revival of nature in spring."
And if that is the nature of the rite which appears
in northern Europe as the harvest supper, it will
also be the nature of the rite as it appears both in
our second group of instances, where the corn is
eaten "as the body of the corn-spirit," and in the
first group, where the dough image or paste idol was
eaten in Mexico as the flesh and bones of the god.
That this line of thought runs through Dr. Frazer's
Golden Bough, in its second edition, is indicated by
the fact that the rite is spoken of throughout as a

sacrament. That the Mexican rite as described in our first group is sacramental, is clear. Of the rites which form our second group of instances, Dr. Frazer says that the corn-spirit, or god, "is killed in the person of his representative and eaten sacramentally," and that "the new corn is itself eaten sacramentally; that is, as the body of the corn-spirit" (p. 318). Of the North European rites, again, he says, "the animal is slain and its flesh and blood are partaken of by the harvesters" — "these customs bring out clearly the sacramental character of the harvest supper" — "as a substitute for the real flesh of the divine being, bread or dumplings are made in his image and eaten sacramentally." Finally, even when speaking of the Australians as men who have no gods to worship, and with whom the rite is pure and unadulterated magic, he yet describes the rite as a sacrament.

Now if, on the one hand, from its beginning amongst the Australians to the form which it finally took amongst the Mexicans the rite is, as Dr. Frazer systematically calls it, a sacrament; and if, on the other, it is, in Dr. Frazer's words, "a magical rite intended to assure the revival of nature in spring," then the conclusion which the reader cannot help drawing is that a sacrament, or this sacrament at least, is in its origin, and in its nature throughout, a piece of magic. Religion is but magic written in different characters; and for those who can interpret them it spells the same thing. But though this is the conclusion to which Dr. Frazer's argument leads, and to which in the first edition of his *Golden Bough* it clearly seemed to point; in the preface to the second edition he formally disavows it. He recognises that religion does not spring from magic, but is fundamentally opposed to it. A sacrament, therefore, we may infer, cannot be a piece of magic. The Australian sacrament, therefore, as Dr. Frazer calls it, cannot, we should be inclined to say, be a piece of magic. But Dr. Frazer still holds that the Australian rite or sacrament is pure magic — religious it cannot be, for in Dr. Frazer's view the Australians know no religion and have no gods.

Now if the rite as it occurs in Australia is pure magic, and if religion is not a variety of magic but fundamentally different from it, then the rite which, as it occurs everywhere else, is religious, cannot be derived from, or a variety of, the Australian piece of magic; and the spring and harvest customs which are found in Australia cannot be "based on the

same ancient modes of thought or form part of the
same primitive heathendom" as the sacramental
rites which are found everywhere else in the world.
The solemn annual eating of the totem plant or
animal in Australia must have a totally different
basis from that on which the sacrament and communion stands in every other part of the globe:
in Australia it is based on magic, elsewhere on that
which is, according to Dr. Frazer, fundamentally
different and opposed to magic, viz. religion. Before,
however, we commit ourselves to this conclusion,
we may be allowed to ask, What is it that compels
us thus to sever the Australian from the other forms
of the rite? The reply would seem to be that,
whereas the other forms are admittedly religious,
the Australian is "a magical rite intended to assure
the revival of nature in spring." Now, if that were
really the nature of the Australian rite, we might
have to accept the conclusion to which we hesitate
to commit ourselves. But, as a matter of fact, the
Australian rite is not intended to assure the revival
of nature in spring, and has nothing magical about
it. It is perfectly true that in spring in Australia
certain proceedings are performed which are based
upon the principle that like produces like; and

that these proceedings are, by students of the science of religion, termed — perhaps incorrectly — magical. But these spring customs are quite different from the harvest customs; and it is the harvest customs which constitute the link between the rite in Australia and the rite in the rest of the world. The crucial question, therefore, is whether the Australian harvest rite is magical, or is even based on the principle that like produces like. And the answer is that it is plainly not. The harvest rite in Australia consists, as we know it now, simply in the fact that at the appointed time a little of the totem plant or animal is solemnly and sparingly eaten by the headman of the totem. The solemnity with which the rite is performed is unmistakable, and may well be termed religious. And no attempt even, so far as I am aware, has been made to show that this solemn eating is regarded as magic by the performers of the rite, or how it can be so regarded by students of the science of religion. Until the attempt is made and made successfully, we are more than justified in refusing to regard the rite as magical; we are bound to refuse to regard it as such. But if the rite is not magical — and à *fortiori* if it is, as Dr. Frazer terms it, sacramental — then it is religious; and the ancient mode of thought, forming part of primitive heathendom, which is at the base of the rite, is the conviction that manifests itself wherever the rite continues to live, viz. that by prayer and sacrifice the worshippers in any community are brought into communion with the god they worship. The rite is, in truth, what Dr. Frazer terms it as it occurs in Australia — a sacrament. But not even in Australia is a sacrament a piece of magic.

In the animistic stage of the evolution of humanity, the only causes man can conceive of are animated things; and, in the presence of any occurrence sufficiently striking to arrest his attention, the questions which present themselves to his mind are, Who did this thing, and why? Occurrences which arrest the attention of the community are occurrences which affect the community; and in a low stage of evolution, when the most pressing of all practical questions is how to live, the occurrences which most effectually arrest attention are those which affect the food supply of the community. If, then, the food supply fails, the occurrence is due to some of the personal, or quasi-personal, powers by whom the community is surrounded; and the reason why such power so acted is found in the wrath which must have actuated him. The situation is abnormal, for famine is abnormal; and it indicates anger and wrath on the part of the power who brought it about. But it also implies that when things go on in the normal way, — when the relations between the spirit and the community are normal, — the attitude of the spirit to the community is peaceable and friendly. Not only, however, does the community desire to renew peaceable and friendly relations, where pestilence or famine show that they have been disturbed: the community also desires to benefit by them when they are in their normal condition. The spirits that can disturb the normal conditions by sending pestilence or famine can also assist the community in undertakings, the success of which is indispensable if the community is to maintain its existence; for instance, those undertakings on which the food supply of the community depends. Hence the petitions which are put up at seed time, or, in the pre-agricultural period, at seasons analogous to seed time. Hence, also, the rites at harvest time or the analogous season, rites which are instituted and developed for the purpose of maintaining friendly relation and communion between the community, and the spirit whose favour is sought and whose anger is dreaded by the community. Such sacrificial rites may indeed be interpreted as the making of gifts to the gods; and they do, as a matter of fact, often come so to be regarded by those who perform them. From this undeniable fact the inference may then be drawn, and by many students of the science of religion it is inferred, that from the beginning there was in such sacrificial rites no other intention than to bribe the god or to purchase his favour and the good things he had to give. But the inference, which, when properly limited, has some truth in it, becomes misleading when put forward as being the whole truth. Unless there were some truth in it, the rite of sacrifice could never have developed into the form which was denounced by the Hebrew prophets and mercilessly exposed by Plato. But had that been the whole truth, the rite would have been incapable of discharging the really religious function which it has in its history fulfilled. That function has been to place and maintain the society which practises it in communion with its god. Doubtless in the earliest stages of the history of the rite, the communion thus felt to be established was prized and was mainly sought for the external blessings which were believed

to follow from it, or, as a means to avert the public
disasters which a breach of communion entailed.
Doubtless it was only by degrees, and by slow
degrees, that the communion thus established came
to be regarded as being in itself the end which the
rite of sacrifice was truly intended to attain. But
the communion of the worshippers with their god
was not a purpose originally foreign to the rite, and
which, when introduced, transformed the rite from
what it at first was into something radically different.
On the contrary, it was present, even though not
prominent or predominant, from the beginning;
and the rite, as a religious institution, followed
different lines of evolution, according as the one
aspect or the other was developed. Where the aspect under which the sacrificial rite was regarded
was that the offering was a gift made to the deity
in order to secure some specified temporal advantage,
the religious value of the rite diminished to the
vanishing point in the eyes both of those who, like
Plato, could see the intrinsic absurdity of pretending
to make gifts to Him from whom alone all good
things come, and of those who felt that the sacrificial
rite so conceived did not afford the spiritual communion for which they yearned. Where even the

sacrificial rite was regarded as a means whereby communion between the worshipper and his god was attained or maintained, the emphasis might be thrown on the rite and its due performance rather than on the spiritual communion of which it was the condition. That is to say, with the growth of formalism attention was concentrated on the ritual and correspondingly withdrawn from the prayer which, from the beginning, had been of the essence of the rite. By the rite of sacrifice the community had always been brought into the presence of the god it worshipped; and, in the prayers then offered on behalf of the society, the society had been brought into communion with its god. From that communion it was possible to fall away, even though the performance of the rite was maintained. The very object of that communion might be misinterpreted and mistaken to be a means merely to temporal blessings for the community, or even to personal advantages for the individual. Or the punctilious performance of each and every detail of the rite might tend to become an end in itself and displace the spiritual communion, the attainment of which had been from the beginning the highest, even if not the only or the most prominent, end which the rite might subserve. The difference between the possibilities which the rite might have realised and the actual purposes for which it had come to be used before the birth of Christ is a difference patent to the most casual observer of the facts. The dissatisfaction felt alike by Plato and the Hebrew prophets with the rite as it had come to be practised may be regarded, if we choose so to regard it, as the necessary consequence of pre-existing facts, and as necessarily entailing the rejection or the reconstitution of the rite. As a matter of history, the rite was reconstituted and not rejected; and as reconstituted it became the central fact of the Christian religion. It became the means whereby, through Christ, all men might be brought to God. We may say, if we will, that a new meaning was put into the rite, or that its true meaning was now made manifest. The facts themselves clearly indicate that from the beginning the rite was the means whereby a society sought or might seek communion with its god. They also indicate that the rite of animal sacrifice came to be found insufficient as a means. It was through our Lord that mankind learned what sacrifice was needed — learned to "offer and present unto thee. O Lord, ourselves, our souls and bodies, to be a reasonable, holy and lively sacrifice unto thee." That is the sacrifice Christ showed us the example of; that is the example which the missionary devotes himself to follow and to teach.

MORALITY

In this lecture I propose to consider the question whether morality is based on religion or religion on morality. It is a question which may be approached from the point of view either of philosophy or of history. Quite recently it has been treated from the former point of view by Professor Höffding in *The Philosophy of Religion* (translated into English, 1906); and from the point of view of the history of morality by Mr. Hobhouse in his *Morals in Evolution* (1906). It may, of course, also be quite properly approached from the point of view of the history of religion; and from whatever standpoint it is treated, the question is one of importance for the missionary, both because of its intrinsic interest for the philosophy of religion, and because its discussion is apt to proceed on a mistaken view of facts in the history of religion. About those facts and their meaning, the missionary, who is to be properly equipped for his work, should be in no doubt: a right view and a proper estimate of the facts are essential both for

his practical work and for the theoretical justification of his position.

One answer to the question before us is that
morality is the basal fact — the bottom fact: if we
regard the question historically, we shall find that
morality came first and religion afterwards; and,
even if that were not so, we should find that as a
matter of logic and philosophy religion presupposes
morality — religion may, for a time, be the lever
that moves the world, but it would be powerless if
it had not a fulcrum, and that fulcrum is morality.
So long and so far as religion operates beneficially
on the world, it does so simply because it supports
and reënforces morality.   But the time is not far
distant, and may even now be come, when morality
no longer requires any support from religion — and
then religion becomes useless, nay! an encum-
brance which must either fall off or be lopped off.
If, therefore, morality can stand by itself, and all
along has not merely stood by itself, but has really
upheld religion, in what is morality rooted?   The
answer is that morality has its roots, not in the command that thou shalt love the Lord thy God with
all thy heart and all thy soul, but in human solidarity, in humanity regarded as a spiritual whole.   To

this conclusion, it is said, the history of recent philosophy has steadily been moving. If the movement had taken place in only one school of philosophic thought, it might have been a movement running into a side-track. But it is the direction taken by schools so different in their presuppositions and their methods as that of Hegel and that of Comte; and it is the undesigned coincidence of their tendency, which at first could never have been surmised, that carries with it a conviction of its correctness. Human solidarity, humanity regarded as a spiritual whole, may be called, as Hegel calls it, self-conscious spirit; or you may call it, as Comte calls it, the Mind of Humanity — it is but the collective wisdom "of a common humanity with a common aim"; and, that being so, morality is rooted, not in the will and the love of a beneficent and omnipotent Providence, but in the self-realising spirit in man setting up its "common aim" at morality. The very conception of a beneficent and omnipotent God — having now done its work as an aid to morality — must now be put aside, because it stands in the way of our recognising what is the real spiritual whole, besides which there is none other spirit, viz. the self-realising spirit in man. That spirit is only realising; it is not yet realised. It is in process of realisation; and the conception of it, as in process of realisation, enables it to be brought into harmony, or rather reveals its inner harmony, with the notion of evolution. There is nothing outside evolution, no being to whom evolution is presented as a spectacle or by whom, as a process, it is directed. "Being itself," as Höffding says (*Problems of Philosophy*, p. 136), "is to be conceived as in process of becoming, of evolution." The spirit in man, as we have just said, is the real spiritual whole, and it is self-realising; it is evolving and progressing both morally and rationally. In Höffding's words "Being itself becomes more rational than before" (*ib.*, p. 137). "Being itself is not ready-made but still incomplete, and rather to be conceived as a continual becoming, like the individual personality and like knowledge" (*ib.*, p. 120). We may say, then, that being is becoming rationalised and moralised as and because the spirit in man realises itself. For a time the process of moralisation and self-realisation was worked by and through the conception of a beneficent and omnipotent god. That conception was, it would seem, a hypothesis, valuable as long it was a working hypothesis, but to be cast aside now that humanitarianism is found more adequate to the facts and more in harmony with the consistent application of the theory of evolution. We have, then, to consider whether it is adequate to the facts, whether, when we regard the facts of the history of religion, we do find that morality comes first and religion later.

"What," Mr. Hobhouse enquires in his *Morals in Evolution* (II, 74), "What is the ethical character of early religion?" and his reply is that "in the first stage we find that spirits, as such, are not concerned with morality." That was also the answer which had previously been given by Professor Höffding, who says in his *Philosophy of Religion:* "in the lowest forms of it . . . religion cannot be said to have any ethical significance" (p. 323). Originally, the gods were "purely natural forces which could be defied or evaded," though eventually they "became ethical powers whom men neither could nor wished to defy" (p. 324). This first stage of early religion seems on the terms of the hypothesis to be supposed to be found in the period of animism and fetichism; and "the primitive conception of spirit" is, Mr. Hobhouse says (II, 16), of something "feeling and thinking like a rather stupid man, and open like him to supplication, exhortation, or intimidation." If that is so, then Professor Höffding may be justified in saying that in the lowest forms of religion "the gods appear as powers on which man is dependent, but not as patterns of conduct or administrators of an ethical world order" (p. 324). Now, in the period termed animistic because inanimate things are supposed to be animated and actuated by spirits, it may be that many or most of such spirits are supposed to feel and think like a rather stupid man, and therefore to be capable of being cajoled, deluded, intimidated, and castigated by the human being who desires to make use of them. But it is not all such spirits that are worshipped then. Indeed, it is impossible, Mr. Hobhouse says (II, 15), that any such spirit could be "an object of worship in our sense of the term." Worship implies the superiority of the .object worshipped to the person worshipping. But, though not an object of worship in our sense of the term, the spirit that could be deluded, intimidated, and castigated was, according to Mr. Hobhouse, "the object of a religious cult" on the part of the man who believed that he could and did intimidate and castigate the spirit. Probably, however, most students of the science of religion would agree that a cult which included or allowed intimidation and castigation of the object of the cult was as little entitled to be termed religious as it is to be called worship. In the period of animism, then, either there was no religious cult, no worship in our sense of the term; or, if there was religion, then the spirit worshipped was worshipped as a being higher than man. Whether man has at any time been without religion is a question on which there is here no need to enter. The allegation we are now considering is that whenever religion does appear, then in its first and earliest stage it is not concerned with morality; and the ground for that allegation is that the spirits of the animistic period have nothing to do with morality or conduct. Now, it may be that these spirits which animate inanimate things are not concerned with morality; but then neither are they worshipped, nor is the relation between them and man religious. Religion implies a god; and a spirit to be a god must have worshippers, a community of worshippers — whether that community be a nation, a tribe, or a family. Further, it is as the protector of the interests of that community — however small — that the god is worshipped by the community. The indispensable condition of religion is the existence of a community;

and from the beginning man must have lived in some
sort of community, — whether a family or a horde, —
for the period of helpless infancy is so long in the case
of human beings that without some sort of permanent community the race could not be perpetuated.
The indispensable condition of religion, therefore,
has always existed from the time when man was
man. Further, whatever the form of community
in which man originally dwelt, it was only in the
community and by means of the community that
the individual could exist — that is to say, if the
interest of any one individual conflicted or was supposed to conflict with the interests of the community, then the interests of the community must prevail, if the community was to exist. Here, then,
from the beginning we have the second condition
indispensable for the existence of religion, viz. the
possibility that the conduct of some member of the
community might not be the conduct required by
the interests or supposed interests of the community,
and prescribed by the custom of the. community.
In the case of such divergence of interests and conduct, the being worshipped by the community was
necessarily, as being the god of the community, and
receiving the worship of the community, on the side

of the community and against the member who
violated the custom of the community. But, at this
period in the history of humanity, the morality of
the community was the custom of the community;
and the god of the community from the first necessarily upheld the custom, that is, the morality of the
community. Spirits "as such," that is to say, spirits
which animated inanimate things but which were not
the protectors of any human community, were, for
the very reason that they were not the gods of any
community, "not concerned with morality." Spirits,
however, which were the protectors of a community
necessarily upheld the customs and therefore the
morality of the community; they were not "without
ethical significance." It was an essential part of
the very conception of such spirits — of spirits stand-
ing in this relation to the community — that they
were "ethical powers." Höffding's dictum that
"the gods appear as powers on which man is dependent, but not as patterns of conduct or administrators of an ethical world order" (p. 323), overlooks
the fact that in the earliest times not only are gods
powers on which man is dependent, but powers
which enforce the conduct required by the custom
of the community and sanction the ethical order as

far as it has then been revealed. The fact that "the worship of the family, of the clan, or of the nation is shared in by all," not merely "helps to nourish a feeling of solidarity which may acquire ethical significance," as Höffding says (p. 325), it creates a solidarity which otherwise would not exist. If there were no worship shared in by all, there would be no religious solidarity; and, judging from the very general, if not universal, occurrence of religion in the lowest races as well as the highest, we may conjecture that without religious solidarity a tribe found it hard or impossible to survive in the struggle for existence. That religious solidarity however is not, as Höffding suggests, something which may eventually "acquire ethical significance"; it is in its essence and from the beginning the worship of a god who punishes the community for the ethical transgression of its members, because they are not merely violations of the custom of the community, but offences against him. When Höffding says (p. 328) "religious faith . . . assumes an independent human ethic, which has, as a matter of fact, developed historically under the practical influence of the ethical feeling of man," he seems to overlook the fact that as a matter of history human ethics have always been based — rightly or wrongly — on religious faith, that moral transgressions have always been regarded as not merely wrongs done to a man's neighbour, but also as offences against the god or gods of the community, that the person suffering from foul wrong for which he can get no human redress has always appealed from man to God, and that the remorse of the wrong-doer who has evaded human punishment has always taken shape in the fear of what God may yet do.

Those who desire to prove that at the present day morality can exist apart from religion, and that in the future it will do so, finding its basis in humanitarianism and not in religion, are moved to show that as a matter of historic fact religion and morality have been things apart. We have examined the assertion that religion in its lowest forms is not concerned with morality; and we have attempted to show that the god of a community, or the spirit worshipped by a community, is necessarily a being conceived as concerned with the interests of the community and as hostile to those who violate the customs — which is to transgress the morality — of the community. But even if this be admitted, it may still be said that it does not in the least disprove the assertion that morality existed before religion did. The theory we are examining freely admits that religion is supposed, in certain stages of the history of humanity, to reënforce morality and to be necessary in the interest of morals, though eventually it is found that morality needs no such support; and not only needs now no such support but never did need it; and the fact that it did not need it is shown by demonstrating the existence of morality before religion existed. If, then, it be admitted that religion from the moment it first appeared reënforced morality, and did not pass through a non-moral period first, still morality may have existed before religion was evolved, and must have so existed if morality and religion are things essentially apart. What evidence then is there on the point? We find Mr. Hobhouse saying (I, 80) that "at almost, if not quite, the lowest stages" of human development there are "certain actions which are resented as involving the community as a whole in misfortune and danger. These include, besides actual treason, conduct which brings upon the people the wrath of God, or of certain spirits, or which violates some mighty and mysterious taboo. The actions most frequently regarded in this light are certain breaches of the marriage law and witchcraft."

These offences, we are told (*ib.*, 82), endanger the community itself, and the punishment is "prompted by the sense of a danger to the whole community." Here, then, from the beginning we find that offences against the common good are punished, not simply as such, but as misconduct bringing on the community, and not merely on the offender, the wrath of gods or spirits. In other words — Mr. Hobhouse's words, p. 119 — "in the evolution of public justice, we find that at the outset the community interferes mainly on what we may call supernatural grounds only with actions which are regarded as endangering its own existence." We may then fairly say that if the community inflicts punishments mainly on supernatural grounds from the time when the evolution of public justice first begins, then morality from its very beginning was reënforced — indeed prompted — by religion. The morality was indeed only the custom of the community; but violation of the custom was from the beginning regarded as a religious offence and was punished on supernatural grounds.

The view that morality and religion are essentially distinct, that morality not only can stand alone, without support from religion, but has in reality always stood without such support — however much the fact has been obscured by religious prepossessions — this view receives striking confirmation from the current and generally accepted theory of the origin and nature of justice. That theory traces the origin of justice back to the feeling of resentment experienced by the individual against the particular cause of his pain (Westermarck, *Origin and Development of the Moral Ideas*, I, 22). Resentment leads to retaliation and takes the form of revenge. Vengeance, at first executed by the person injured (or by his kin, if he be killed), comes eventually, if slowly, to be taken out of the hands of the person injured or his avengers, and to be exercised by the State in the interests of the community and in furtherance, not of revenge, but of justice and the good of society. Thus not only the origin of justice, but the whole course of its growth and development, is entirely independent of religion and religious considerations. Throughout, the individual and society are the only parties involved; the gods do not appear — or, if they do appear, they are intrusive and superfluous. If this be the true view of the history and nature of justice, it may — and probably must — be the truth about the whole of morality and not only about justice. We have but to follow Dr. Westermarck (*ib.*, p. 21) in grouping the moral emotions under the two heads of emotions of approval and emotions of disapproval, we have but to note with him that both groups belong to the class of retributive emotions, and we see that the origin and history of justice are typical of the origin and history of morals: morality in general, just as much as justice in particular, both originates independently of religion and developes — where moral progress is made — independently of religion.

Let us now proceed to examine this view of the relation of religion and morality and to consider whether their absolute independence of each other is historic fact. It traces back justice to the feeling of resentment experienced by the individual; but if the individual ever existed by himself and apart from society, there could neither then be justice nor anything analogous to justice, for justice implies, not merely a plurality of individuals, but a society; it is a social virtue. The individual existing by himself and apart from society is not a historic fact but an impossible abstraction — a conception essentially false because it expresses something which neither exists nor has existed nor could possibly exist. The origin of justice — or of any virtue — cannot be found in the impossible and self-contradictory conception of the individual existing apart from society; it cannot be found in a mere plurality of such individuals: it can only be found in a society — whether that society have the organisation of a family, a tribe, or a nation. Justice in particular and morality in general, like religion, imply the existence of a society; neither is a merely individual affair. Justice is, as Mr. Hobhouse states, "public action taken for the sake of public safety" (I, 83): it is, from the outset of its history, public action; and back of that we cannot go, for the individual did not, as a matter of history, exist before society, and could not so have existed.

In the next place, justice is not the resentment of any individual, it is the sentiment of the community expressing itself in public action, taken not for the sake of any individual, but for the sake of public safety. Its object from the beginning is not the gratification of individual resentment, but the safety and welfare of the community which takes common action. Proof of this, if proof were needed, would be found in the fact that the existence of the individual, as such, is not recognised. Not only does the community which has suffered in the wrong done to any of its members take action as a community; it proceeds, not against the individual who has inflicted the wrong, but against the community to which he belongs. "The wrong done," is, as Mr. Hobhouse says (I, 91), "the act of the family or clan and may be avenged on any member of that family or clan." There is collective responsibility for the wrong done, just as there is collective responsibility for righting it.

If, now, we enquire, What are the earliest offences against which public action is taken? and why? we may remember that Mr. Hobhouse has stated them to be witchcraft and breaches of the marriage law; and that the punishment of those offences corresponds, as he has said, "roughly to our own administration of justice" (I, 81). Now, in the case of breaches of the marriage laws — mating with a cousin on the mother's side instead of with a cousin on the father's side, marrying into a forbidden class — it is obvious that there is no individual who has suffered injury and that there is no individual to experience resentment. It is the community that suffers or is expected to suffer; and it expects to suffer, because it, in the person of one of its members, has offended. Collectively it is responsible for the misdeeds of its members. Whom, then, has it offended? To whom is it responsible? Who will visit it with punishment, unless it makes haste to set itself right? The answer given by a certain tribe of the Sea Dyaks makes the matter clear: they, Mr. St. John tells us in his *Life in the Forests of the Far East* (I, 63, quoted by Westermarck, I, 49), "are of opinion that an unmarried girl proving with child must be offensive to the superior powers, who, instead of always chastising the individual, punish the tribe by misfortunes happening to its members. They therefore on the discovery of the pregnancy fine the lovers, and sacrifice a pig to propitiate offended heaven, and to avert that sickness or those misfortunes that might otherwise follow." That is, of course, only one instance. But we may safely say that the marriage law is generally ascribed to the ordinance of the gods, even in the lowest tribes, and that breaches of it are offences against heaven.

It is unnecessary to prove, it need only be mentioned, that witchcraft is conspicuously offensive to the religious sentiment, and is punished as an offence against the god or gods. When, then, we consider the origin and nature of justice, not from

an abstract and *à priori* point of view, but in the light
of historic fact, so far from finding that it originates
and operates in complete independence of religion,
we discover that from the beginning the offences
with which the justice of the primitive community
deals are offences, not against the community, but
against heaven. "In the evolution of public justice," as Mr. Hobhouse says, "at the outset the community interferes mainly on what we may call
supernatural grounds." From the beginning misdeeds are punished, not merely as wrongs done to
society, but as wrong done to the gods and as wrong-
doing for which the community collectively is responsible to the gods. Justice from the beginning is
not individual resentment, but "public action taken
for the public safety." It is not, as Mr. Hobhouse
calls it, "revenge guided and limited by custom."
It is the customary action of the community taken
to avert divine vengeance. The action taken assumes
in extreme cases the form of the death penalty; but
its usual form of action is that of taboo.

If the origin of justice is to be sought in something
that is not justice, if justice in particular and morality in general are to be treated as having been
evolved out of something which was in a way different

from them and yet in a way must have contained them, inasmuch as they came forth from it, we shall do well to look for that something, not in the unhistorical, unreal abstraction of an imaginary individual, apart from society, but in society itself when it is as yet not clearly conscious of the justice and morality at work within it.   Such a stage in the development of society is, I think, to be discerned.

We have seen that, "at almost, if not quite, the lowest stages" of human development, there is something which, according to Mr. Hobhouse, corresponds "roughly to our own administration of justice" (I, 81).   But this rough justice implies conscious, deliberate action on the part of the community.   It implies that the community as such makes some sort of enquiry into what can be the cause of the misfortunes which are befalling it; and that, having found out the person responsible, it deliberately takes the steps it deems necessary for putting itself right with the supernatural power that has sent the sickness or famine.   Now, such conscious, purposive, deliberate action may and probably does take place at almost the lowest stage of development of society; but not, we may surmise, at quite the lowest.   What eventually is done consciously and deliberately is probably done in the first place much more summarily and automatically. And — in quite the lowest stage of social development — it is by means of the action of taboo that summary and automatic punishment for breaches of the custom of the community is inflicted. Its action is automatic and immediate: merely to come in contact with the forbidden thing is to become tabooed yourself; and so great is the horror and dread of such contact, even if made unwittingly, that it is capable of causing, when discovered, death. Like the justice, however, of which it is the forerunner, it does not result always in death, nor does it produce that effect in most cases. But what it does do is to make the offender himself taboo and as infectious as the thing that rendered him taboo. Here, too, the action of taboo, in excommunicating the offender, anticipates, or rather foreshadows, the action of justice when it excludes the guilty person from the community and makes of him an outlaw. Again, in the rough justice found at almost, though not quite, the lowest stages, the earliest offences of which official notice, so to speak, is taken, are offences for which the punishment — disease or famine, etc. — falls on the community as a whole, because the community, in the person of one of its members, has offended as a whole against heaven. In the earlier stage of feeling, also, which survives where taboo prevails, it is the community as a whole which may be infected, and which must suffer if the offender is allowed to spread the infection; it is the community, as a whole, which is concerned to thrust out the guilty person — every one shuns him because he is taboo. Thus, in this the earliest stage, the offender against the custom of the community is outlawed just as effectively as in later stages of social development. But no formal sentence is pronounced; no meeting of the men or the elders of the community is held to try the offender; no reason is given or sought why the offence should thus be punished. The operation of taboo is like that of the laws of nature: the man who eats poisonous food dies with no reason given. A reason may eventually be found by science, and is eventually discovered, though the process of discovery is slow, and many mistakes are made, and many false reasons are given before the true reason is found. So, too, the true reason for the prohibition of many of the things, which the community feels to be forbidden and pronounced to be taboo, is found, with the progress of society — when it does progress, which is not always — to be that they are immoral and irreligious, though here, too, many mistakes are made before true morality and true religion are found. But at the outset no reason is given: the things are simply offensive to the community and are tabooed as such. We, looking back at that stage in the evolution of society, can see that amongst the things thus offensive and tabooed are some which, in later stages, are equally offensive, but are now forbidden for a reason that can be formulated and given, viz. that they are offences against the law of morality and the law of God. That reason, at the outset of society, may scarcely have been consciously present to the mind of man: progress, in part at least, has consisted in the discovery of the reasons of things. But that man did from the beginning avoid some of the things which are forbidden by morality and religion, and that those things were taboo to him, is beyond the possibility of doubt. Nor can it be doubted that in the prohibition and punishment of them there was inchoate justice and inchoate religion. Such prohibition was due to the collective action and expressed the collective feeling of the community as a whole. And it is from such social action and feeling that justice, I suggest, has been evolved — not from the feeling of resentment experienced by the individual as an individual. Personal resentment and personal revenge may have stimulated justice to action. But, by the hypothesis we have been examining, they were not justice. Neither have they been transformed into justice: they still exist as something distinct from justice and capable of perverting it.

The form which justice takes in the period which is almost, but not quite, the lowest stage of human evolution is the sense of the collective responsibility of the community for all its actions, that is to say, for the acts of all its members. And that responsibility in its earliest shape is felt to be a responsibility to heaven, to the supernatural powers that send disease and famine upon the community. In those days no man sins to himself alone, just as, in still earlier days, no man could break a taboo without becoming a source of danger to the whole community. The wrong-doer has offended against the supernatural powers and has brought down calamity upon the community. He is therefore punished, directly as an offender against the god of the community, and indirectly for having involved the com-

munity in suffering. In Dr. Westermarck's words
(I, 194), there is "genuine indignation against the
offender, both because he rebels against God, and
because he thereby exposes the whole community
to supernatural dangers." But though society for
many long centuries continues to punish rebellion
against God, still in the long run it ceases, or tends
to cease, doing so. Its reason for so ceasing is interpreted differently by different schools of thought.
On the one hand, it is said in derision, let the gods
punish offences against the gods — the implication
being that there are no such offences to punish,
because there is no god. On the other hand, it is
said, "I will repay, saith the Lord" — the implication being that man may not assume to be the minister of divine vengeance. If, then, we bear in mind
that the fact may be interpreted in either of these
different ways, we shall not fall into the fallacy
of imagining that the mere existence of the fact
suffices to prove either interpretation to be true.
Yet this fallacy plays its part in lending fictitious
support to the doctrine that morality is in no wise
dependent upon religion. The offences now punished by law, it is argued, are no longer punished
as offences against religion, but solely as offences

against the good of the community.   To this argument the reply is that men believe the good of the community to be the will of God, and do not believe murder, theft, adultery, etc., to be merely offences against man's laws.   Overlooking this fact, which is fatal to the doctrine that morality is in no wise dependent on religion, the argument we are discussing proceeds to maintain that the basis for the enforcement of morality by the law is recognised by every one who knows anything of the philosophy of law to be what is good for the community and its members: fraud and violence are punished as such, and not because they are offences against this or that religion.   The fact that the law no longer punishes them as offences against God suffices to show that it is only as offences against humanity that there is any sense, or ever was any sense, in punishing them.   Religion may have reënforced morality very usefully at one time, by making out that moral misdeeds were offences against God, but such arguments are not now required.   The good and the well-being of humanity is in itself sufficient argument.   Humanitarianism is taking the place of religion, and by so doing is demonstrating that morality is, as it always has been, independent of religion; and that in truth religion has built upon it, not it upon religion. As Höffding puts it (p. 328): "Religious faith . . . assumes an independent human ethic developed historically under the practical influence of the ethical feeling of man." That is to say, morality is in Höffding's view independent of religion, and prior to religion, both as a matter of logic and of history. As a matter of history — of the history of religion — this seems to me, for the reasons already given, to be contrary to the facts as they are known. The real reason for maintaining that morality is and must be — and must have been — independent of religion, seems to me to be a philosophical reason. I may give it in Höffding's own words: "What other aims and qualities," he asks (p. 324), "could man attribute to his gods or conceive as divine, but those which he has learnt from his own experience to recognise as the highest?" The answer expected to the question plainly is not merely that it is from experience that man learns, but that man has no experience of God from which he could learn. The answer given by Mr. Hobhouse, in the concluding words of his *Morals in Evolution* is that "the collective wisdom" of man "is all that we directly know of the Divine."

Here, too, no direct access to God is allowed to be possible to man. It is from his experience of other men — perhaps even of himself and his own doings — that man learns all he knows of God: but he has himself no experience of God. Obviously, then, from this humanitarian point of view, what a man goes through in his religious moments is not experience, and we are mistaken if we imagine that it was experience; it is only a misinterpretation of experience. It is on the supposition that we are mistaken, on the assumption that we make a misinterpretation, that the argument is built to prove that morality is and must be independent of religion. Argument to show, or proof to demonstrate, that we had not the experience, or, that we mistook something else for it, is, of course, not forthcoming. But if we hold fast to our conviction, we are told that we are fleeing "to the bosom of faith."

Until some better argument is produced, we may be well content not merely to flee but to rest there.

CHRISTIANITY

THE subject dealt with in this lecture will be the place of Christianity in the evolution of religion; and I shall approach it by considering the place of religion in the evolution of humanity. It will be therefore advisable, indeed necessary, for me to consider what is meant by evolution; and I wish to begin by explaining the point of view from which I propose to approach the three ideas of evolution, of the evolution of humanity and the evolution of religion.

The individual exists, and can only exist, in society. Society cannot exist without individuals as members thereof; and the individual cannot exist save in society. From this it follows that from one point of view the individual may be regarded as a means — a means by which society attains its end or purpose: every one of us has his place or function in society; and society thrives according as each member performs his function and discharges his duty. From another point of view

the individual may be regarded as an end. If
man is a social animal, if men live in society, it
is because so alone can a man do what is best for
himself: it is by means of society that he realises
his end. It is then from this proposition, viz. that
the individual is both a means and an end, that
I wish to approach the idea of evolution.

I will begin by calling attention to the fact that
that proposition is true both statically, that is to
say, is true of the individual's position in a community, and is also true dynamically, that is to say,
is true of his place in the process of evolution. On
the former point, that the proposition is true statically, of the position of the individual in the community, I need say but little. In moral philosophy
it is the utilitarian school which has particularly
insisted upon this truth. That school has steadily
argued that, in the distribution of happiness or of
the good, every man is to count as one, and nobody
to count as more than one — that is to say, in the
community the individual is to be regarded as the
end. The object to be aimed at is not happiness
in general and no one's happiness in particular,
but the happiness of each and every individual.
It is the individual and his happiness which is the

end, for the sake of which society exists and to which it is the means; otherwise the individual might derive no benefit from society. But if the truth that the individual is an end as well as a means is recognised by moral philosophy, that truth has also played at least an equally important part in political philosophy. It is the very breath of the cry for liberty, equality, and fraternity, — a cry wrung out from the heart of man by the system of oppression which denied that the ordinary citizen had a right to be anything but a means for procuring enjoyment to the members of the ruling class. The truth that any one man — whatever his place in society, whatever the colour of his skin — has as much right as any other to be treated as an end and that no man was merely a means to the enjoyment or happiness or well-being of another, was the charter for the emancipation of slaves. It is still the magna charta for the freedom of every member of the human race. No man is or can be a chattel — a thing existing for no other purpose than to subserve the interests of its owner and to be a means to his ends. But though from the truth that the individual is in himself an end as well as a means. it follows that all men have the right to freedom, it does not follow as a logical inference that all men are equal as means — as means to the material happiness or to the moral improvement of society.

I need not further dwell upon the fact that statically as regards the relations of men to one another in society at any moment, the truth is fully recognised that the individual is not merely a means to the happiness or well-being of others, but is also in himself an end. But when we consider the proposition dynamically, when we wish to find out the part it has played as one of the forces at work in evolution, we find that its truth has been far from fully recognised — partly perhaps because utilitarianism dates from a time when evolution, or the bearing of it, was not understood. But the truth is at least of as great importance dynamically as it is statically. And on one side, its truth and the importance of its truth has been fully developed: that the individual is a means to an end beyond him; and that, dynamically, he has been and is a factor in evolution, and as a factor merely a means and nothing else — all this has been worked out fully, if not to excess. The other side of the truth, the fact that the individual is always an end, has, however,

been as much neglected by the scientific evolutionist
as it was by the slave-driver: he has been liable
to regard men as chattels, as instruments by which
the work of evolution is carried on. The work has
got to be done (by men amongst other animals and
things), things have to be evolved, evolution must go
on. But, why? and for whom? with what purpose
and for whose benefit? with what end? are questions which science leaves to be answered by those
people who are foolish enough to ask them. Science
is concerned simply with the individual as a means,
as one of the means, whereby evolution is carried
on; and doubtless science is justified — if only
on the principle of the division of labour — in con-
fining itself to the department of enquiry which
it takes in hand and in refusing to travel beyond it.
Any theory of man, therefore, or of the evolution
of humanity, which professes to base itself strictly
on scientific fact and to exclude other considerations as unscientific and therefore as unsafe material
to build on, will naturally, and perhaps necessarily,
be dominated by the notion that the individual
exists as a factor in evolution, as one of the means
by which, and not as in any sense the end for which,
evolution is carried on.

Such seems to be the case with the theory of humanitarianism. It bases itself upon science, upon experience, and rules out communion with God as not being a scientific fact or a fact of experience at all. Based upon science, it is a theory which seeks amongst other things to assign to religion its place in the evolution of humanity. According to the theory, the day of religion is over, its part played out, its function in the evolution of humanity discharged. According to this theory, three stages may be discerned in the evolution of humanity when we regard man as a moral being, as an ethical consciousness. Those three stages may be characterised first as custom, next religion, and finally humanitarianism.

By the theory, in the first stage — that of custom — the spirits to whom cult is paid are vindictive. In the second stage — that of religion — man, having attained to a higher morality, credits his gods with that higher morality. In the third stage — that of humanitarianism — he finds that the gods are but lay figures on which the robes of righteousness have been displayed that man alone can wear — when he is perfect. He is not yet perfect. If he were, the evolution of humanity would be attained — whereas at present it is as yet in process. The end of evolution is not yet attained: it is to establish, in some future generation, a perfect humanity. For that end we must work; to it we may know that, as a matter of scientific evolution, we are working. On it, we may be satisfied, man will not enter in our generation.

Now this theory of the evolution of humanity, and of the place religion takes in that evolution, is in essential harmony with the scientific treatment of the evolution theory, inasmuch as it treats of the individual solely as an instrument to something other than himself, as a means of producing a state of humanity to which he will not belong. But if the assumption that the individual is always a means and never an end in himself be false, then a theory of the evolution of man (as an ethical consciousness) which is based on that wrong assumption will itself be wrong. If each individual is an end, as valuable and as important as any other individual; if each counts for one and not less than any one other, — then his end and his good cannot lie in the perfection of some future generation. In that case, his end would be one that *ex hypothesi* he could never enjoy, a rest into which he could never enter;

and consequently it would be an irrational end, and could not serve as a basis for a rationalist theory of ethics. Man's object (to be a rational object) must have reference to a society of which he may be a member. The realisation of his object, therefore, cannot be referred to a stage of society yet to come, on earth, after he is dead, — a society of which he, whether dead or annihilated, could not be a member. If, then, the individual's object is to be a rational object, as the humanitarian or rationalist assumes, then that end must be one in which he can share; and therefore cannot be in this world. Nor can that end be attained by doing man's will — for man's will may be evil, and regress as well as progress is a fact in the evolution of humanity; its attainment, therefore, must be effected by doing God's will.

The truth that the individual is an end as well as a means is, I suggest, valuable in considering the dynamics as well as the statics of society. At least, it saves one from the self-complacency of imagining that one's ancestors existed with no other end and for no higher purpose than to produce — me; and if the golden days anticipated by the theory of humanitarianism ever arrive, it is to be supposed that the men of that time will find it just as intolerable and revolting as we do now, to believe that past generations toiled and suffered for no other reason, for no other end, and to no other purpose than that their successors should enter into the fruits of their labour. In a word, the theory that in the evolution of man as an ethical consciousness, as a moral being, religion is to be superseded by humanitarianism, is only possible so long as we deny or ignore the fact that the individual is an end and not merely a means.

We will therefore now go on to consider the evolution of religion from the point of view that the individual is in himself an end as well as a means. If, of the world religions, we take that which is the greatest, as measured by the number of its adherents, viz. Buddhism, we shall see that, tried by this test, it is at once found wanting. The object at which Buddhism proclaims that man should aim is not the development, the perfection, and the realisation of the individual to the fullest extent: it is, on the contrary, the utter and complete effacement of the individual, so that he is not merely absorbed, but absolutely wiped out, in *nirvana*. In the *atman*, with which it is the duty of man to seek to identify himself, the individuality of man does not survive:

it simply ceases to be. Now this obliteration of his existence may seem to a man in a certain mood desirable; and that mood may be cultivated, as indeed Buddhism seeks to cultivate it, systematically. But here it is that the inner inconsistency, the self-contradictoriness of Buddhism, becomes patent. The individual, to do anything, must exist. If he is to desire nothing save to cease to exist, he must exist to do that. But the teaching of Buddhism is that this world and this life is illusion — and further, that the existence of the individual self is precisely the most mischievous illusion, that illusion above all others from which it is incumbent on us to free ourselves. We are here for no other end than to free ourselves from that illusion. Thus, then, by the teaching of Buddhism there is an end, it may be said, for the individual to aim at. Yes! but by the same teaching there is no individual to aim at it — individual existence is the most pernicious of all illusions. And further, by the teaching, the final end and object of religion is to get rid of an individual existence, which does not exist to be got rid of, and which it is an illusion to believe in. In fine, Buddhism denies that the individual is either an end or a means, for it denies the existence of the individual, and contradicts itself in that denial. The individual is not an end — the happiness or immortality, the continued existence, of the individual is not to be aimed at. Neither is he a means, for his very existence is an illusion, and as such is an obstacle or impediment which has to be removed, in order that he who is not may cease to do what he has never begun to do, viz. to exist.

In Buddhism we have a developed religion — a religion which has been developed by a system of philosophy, but scarcely, as religion, improved by it. If, now, we turn to other religions less highly developed, even if we turn to religions the development of which has been early arrested, which have never got beyond the stage of infantile development, we shall find that all proceed on the assumption that communion between man and God is possible and does occur. In all, the existence of the individual as well as of the god is assumed, even though time and development may be required to realise, even inadequately, what is contained in the assumption. In all, and from the beginning, religion has been a social fact: the god has been the god of the community; and, as such, has repre-

sented the interests of the community. Those
interests have been regarded not merely as other,
but as higher, than the interests of the individual,
when the two have been at variance, for the simple
reason (when the time came for a reason to be
sought and given) that the interests of the community were the will of the community's god.
Hence at all times the man who has postponed his
own interests to those under the sanction of the god
and the community — the man who has respected
and upheld the custom of the community — has
been regarded as the higher type of man, as the better
man from the religious as well as from the moral
point of view; while the man who has sacrificed
the higher interests to the lower, has been punished
— whether by the automatic action of taboo, or
the deliberate sentence of outlawry — as one who,
by breaking custom, has offended against the god
and so brought suffering on the community.

Now, if the interests, whether of the individual
or the community, are regarded as purely earthly,
the divergence between them must be utter and
irreconcileable; and to expect the individual to
forego his own interests must be eventually discovered to be, as it fundamentally is, unreasonable.

If, on the other hand, for the individual to forego
them is (as, in a cool moment, we all recognise it
to be) reasonable, then the interests under the sanction of the god and the community — the higher
interests — cannot be other than, they must be
identical with, the real interests of the individual.
It is only in and through society that the individual
can attain his highest interests, and only by doing
the will of the god that he can so attain them.
Doubtless — despite of logic and feeling — in all
communities all individuals in a greater or less
degree have deliberately preferred the lower to the
higher, and in so doing have been actuated neither
by love of God nor by love of their fellow-man.
But, in so doing, they have at all times, in the latest
as well as the earliest stages of society, been felt to
be breaching the very basis of social solidarity, the
maintenance of which is the will of the God worshipped by society.

From that point of view the individual is regarded
as a means. But he is also in himself an end, in-
trinsically as valuable as any other member of
the community, and therefore an end which society
exists to further and promote. It is impossible,
therefore, that the end, viewed as that which society

as well as the individual aims at, and which society must realise, as far as it can realise it, through the individual, should be one which can only be attained by some future state of society in which he does not exist. "The kingdom of Heaven is within you" and not something to which you cannot attain. God is not far from us at any time. That truth was implicit at all stages in the evolution of religion — consciously recognised, perhaps more, perhaps less, but whether more or less consciously recognised, it was there. That is the conviction implied in the fact that man everywhere seeks God. If he seeks Him in plants, in animals, in stocks or stones, that only shows that man has tried in many wrong directions — not that there is not a right direction. It is the general law of evolution: of a thousand seeds thrown out, perhaps one alone falls into good soil. But the failure of the 999 avails nothing against the fact that the one bears fruit abundantly. What sanctifies the failures is that they were attempts. We indeed may, if we are so selfish and blind, regard the attempts as made in order that we might succeed. Certainly we profit by the work of our ancestors, — or rather we may profit, if we will. But our savage ancestors were themselves ends, and not merely means to our benefit. It is monstrous to imagine that our salvation is bought at the cost of their condemnation. No man can do more than turn to such light as there may be to guide him. "To him that hath, shall be given," it is true — but every man at every time had something; never was there one to whom nothing was given. To us at this day, in this dispensation, much has been given. But ten talents as well as one may be wrapped up: one as well as ten may be put to profit. It is monstrous to say that one could not be, cannot have been, used properly. It was for not using the one talent he had that the unfaithful servant was condemned — not for not having ten to use.

Throughout the history of religion, then, two facts have been implied, which, if implicit at the beginning, have been rendered explicit in the course of its history or evolution. They are, first, the existence of the individual as a member of society, in communion or seeking communion with God; and, next, that while the individual is a means to social ends, society is also a means of which the individual is the end. Neither end — neither that of society nor that of the individual — can be forwarded at the cost of the other; the realisation of each is to be attained only by the realisation of the other. Two consequences then follow with regard to evolution: first, it depends on us; evolution may have helped to make us, but we are helping to make it. Next, the end of evolution is not wholly outside any one of us, but in part is realised in us, or may be, if we so will. That is to say, the true end may be realised by every one of us; for each of us, as being himself an end, is an object of care to God — and not merely those who are to live on earth at the final stage of evolution. If the end is outside us, it is in love of neighbour; if beyond us, it is in God's love. It is just because the end is (or may be) both within us and without us that we are bound up with our fellow-man and God. It is precisely because we are individuals that we are not the be-all and the end-all — that the end is without us. And it is because we are members of a community, that the end is not wholly outside us.

In his *Problems of Philosophy* (p. 163) Höffding says: "The test of the perfection of a human society is: to what degree is every person so placed and treated that he is not only a mere means, but also always at the same time an end?" and he points out that "this is Kant's famous dictum, with another motive than that given to it by him." But if it is reasonable to apply this test to society, regarded from the point of view of statics, it is also reasonable to apply it to society regarded dynamically. If it is the proper test for ascertaining what degree of perfection society at any given moment has attained, it is also the proper test for ascertaining what advance, if any, towards perfection has been made by society between any two periods of its growth, any two stages in its evolution. But the moment we admit the possibility of applying a test to the process of evolution and of discovering to what end the process is moving, we are abandoning science and the scientific theory of evolution. Science formally refuses to consider whether there be any end to which the process of evolution is working: "end" is a category which science declines to apply to its subject-matter. In the interests of knowledge it declines to be influenced by any consideration of what the end aimed at by evolution may be, or whether there be any end aimed at at all. It simply notes what does take place, what is, what has been, and to some extent what may be, the sequence of events — not their object or purpose. And the

science of religion, being a science, restricts itself
in the same way. As therefore science declines to
use the category, "end," progress is an idea impossible for science — for progress is movement towards
an end, the realisation of a purpose and object.
And science declines to consider whether progress
is so much as possible. But, so far as the subject-
matter of the science of religion is concerned, it is
positive (that is to say, it is mere fact of observation) that in religion an end is aimed at, for man
everywhere seeks God and communion with Him.
What the science of religion declines to do is to
pronounce or even to consider whether that end is
possible or not, whether it is in any degree achieved
or not, whether progress is made or not.

But if we do not, as science does, merely constate
the fact that in religion an end is aimed at, viz. that
communion with God which issues in doing His will
from love of Him and therefore of our fellow-man;
if we recognise that end as the end that ought to
be aimed at, — then our attitude towards the whole
process of evolution is changed: it is now a process
with an end — and that end the same for the individual and for society. But at the same time it is
no longer a process determined by mechanical

causes worked by the iron hand of necessity — and therefore it is no longer evolution in the scientific sense; it is no longer evolution as understood by science. It is now a process in which there may or may not be progress made; and in which, therefore, it is necessary to have a test of progress — a test which is to be found in the fact that the individual is not merely a means, but an end. Whether progress is made depends in part on whether there is the will in man to move towards the end proposed; and that will is not uniformly exercised, as is shown by the fact that deterioration as well as advance takes place — regress occurs as well as progress; whole nations, and those not small ones, may be arrested in their religious development. If we look with the eye of the missionary over the globe, everywhere we see arrested development, imperfect communion with God. It may be that in such cases of imperfect communion there is an unconscious or hardly conscious recognition that the form of religion there and then prevalent does not suffice to afford the communion desired. Or, worse still, and much more general, there is the belief that such communion as does exist is all that can exist — that advance and improvement are impossible. From

this state it has been the work of the religious spirit
to wake us, to reveal to us God's will, to make us
understand that it is within us, and that it may,
if we will, work within us. It is as such a revelation of the will of God and the love of God, and as
the manifestation of the personality of God, that
our Lord appeared on earth.

That appearance as a historic fact must take its
place in the order of historic events, and must stand
in relation to what preceded and to what followed
and is yet to follow. In relation to what preceded,
Christianity claims "to be the fulfilment of all that
is true in previous religion" (Illingworth, *Personality: Human and Divine*, p. 75). The making
of that claim assumes that there was some truth in
previous religion, that so far as previous forms were
religious, they were true — a fact that must constantly be borne in mind by the missionary. The
truth and the good inherent in all forms of religion
is that, in all, man seeks after God. The finality
of Christianity lies in the fact that it reveals the
God for whom man seeks. What was true in other
religions was the belief in the possibility of communion with God, and the belief that only as a
member of a society could the individual man attain

to that communion. What is offered by Christianity is a means of grace whereby that communion may be attained and a society in which the individual may attain it.. Christianity offers a means whereby the end aimed at by all religions may be realised. Its finality, therefore, does not consist in its chronological relation to other religions. It is not final because, or in the sense that, it supervened in the order of time upon previous religions, or that it fulfilled only their truth. Other religions have, as a matter of chronology, followed it, and yet others may follow it hereafter. But their chronological order is irrelevant to the question: Which of them best realises the end at which religion, in all its forms, aims? And it is the answer to that question which must determine the finality of any form of religion. No one would consider the fact that Mahommedanism dates some centuries after Christ any proof of its superiority to Christianity. And the lapse of time, however much greater, would constitute no greater proof.

That different forms of religion do realise the end of religion in different degrees is a point on which there is general agreement. Monotheism is pronounced higher than polytheism, ethical religions higher than non-ethical. What differentiates Christianity from other ethical religions and from other forms of monotheism, is that in them religion appears as ancillary to morality, and imposes penalties and rewards with a view to enforce or encourage morality. In them, at their highest, the love of man is for his fellow-man, and usually for himself. Christianity alone makes love of God to be the true basis and the only end of society, both that whereby personality exists and the end in which it seeks its realisation. Therein the Christian theory of society differs from all others. Not merely does it hold that man cannot make himself better without making society better, that development of personality cannot be effected without a corresponding development of society. But it holds that such moral development and improvement of the individual and of society can find no rational basis and has no rational end, save in the love of God.

In another way the Christian theory of society differs from all others. Like all others it holds that the unifying bond of every society is found in worship. Unlike others it recognises that the individual is restricted by existing society, even where that society is based upon a common worship. The

adequate realisation of the potentialities of the individual postulates the realisation of a perfect society,
just as a perfect society is possible only provided
that the potentialities of the individual are realised
to the full. Such perfection, to which both society
and the individual are means, is neither attained
nor possible on earth, even where communion with
God is recognised to be both the true end of society
and the individual, and the only means by which
that end can be attained. Still less is such perfection a possible end, if morality is set above religion,
and the love of man be substituted for the love of
God. In that case the life of the individual upon
earth is pronounced to be the only life of which he
is, or can be, conscious; and the end to which he is
a means is the good of humanity as a whole. Now
human society, from the beginning of its evolution
to its end, may be regarded as a whole, just as the
society existing at any given moment of its evolution
may be regarded as a whole. But if we are to
consider human society from the former point of
view and to see in it, so regarded, the end to which
the individual is a means, then it is clear that, until
perfection is attained in some remote and very
improbable future, the individual members of the

human race will have laboured and not earned their reward, will have worked for an end which they have not attained, and for an end which when, if ever, it is attained, society as a whole will not enjoy. Such an end is an irrational and impossible object of pursuit. Perfection, if it is to be attained by the individual or by society, is not to be attained on earth, nor in man's communion with man. Religion from its outset has been the quest of man for God. It has been the quest of man, whether regarded as an individual or as a member of society. But if that quest is to be realised, it is not to be realised either by society or the individual, regarded as having a mere earthly existence. A new conception of the real nature of both is requisite. Not only must the individual be regarded as continuing to exist after death, but the society of which he is truly a member must be regarded as one which, if it manifests or begins to manifest itself on this earth, requires for its realisation — that is, for perfect communion with God — the postulate that though it manifests itself in this world, it is realised in the next. This new conception of the real nature of society and the individual, involving belief in the communion of the saints, and in the kingdom of Heaven as that which may be in each individual, and therefore must extend beyond each and include all whether in this world or the next — this conception is one which Christianity alone, of all religions, offers to the world.

Religion is the quest of man for God. Man everywhere has been in search of God, peradventure he might find Him; and the history of religion is the history of his search. But the moment we regard the history — the evolution — of religion as a search, we abandon the mechanical idea of evolution: the cause at work is not material or mechanical, but final. The cause is no longer a necessary cause which can only have one result and which, when it operates, must produce that result. Progress is no longer something which must take place, which is the inevitable result of antecedent causes. It is something which may or may not take place and which cannot take place unless effort is made. In a word, it is dependent in part upon man's will — without the action of which neither search can be made nor progress in the search. But though in part dependent upon man's will, progress can only be made so far as man's will is to do God's will. And that is not always, and has not been always, man's will. Hence evolution has not always been progress. Nor is it so now. There have been lapses in civilisation, dark ages, periods when man's love for man has waned *pari passu* with the waning of his love for God. Such lapses there may be yet again. The fall of man may be greater, in the spiritual sense, than it ever yet has been, for man's will is free. But God's love is great, and our faith is in it. If Christianity should cease to grow where it now grows, and cease to spread where it as yet is not, there would be the greater fall. And on us would rest some, at least, of the responsibility. Christianity cannot be stationary: if it stands, let it beware; it is in danger of falling. Between religions, as well as other organisations, there is a struggle for existence. In that struggle we have to fight — for a religion to decline to fight is for that religion to die. The missionary is not engaged in a work of supererogation, something with which we at home have no concern. We speak of him as in the forefront of the battle. We do not usually or constantly realise that it is our battle he is fighting — that his defeat, if he were defeated, would be the beginning of the end for us; that on his success our fate depends. The metaphor of the missionary as an out-

post sounds rather picturesque when heard in a sermon, — or did so sound the first time it was used, I
suppose, — but it is not a mere picture; it is the
barest truth. The extent to which we push our out-
posts forward is the measure of our vitality, of how
much we have in us to do for the world. Six out of
seven of Christendom's missionaries come from the
United States of America. Until I heard that from
the pulpit of Durham Cathedral, I had rather a
horror of big things and a certain apprehension
about going to a land where bigness, rather than the
golden mean, seemed to be taken as the standard of
merit. But from that sermon I learnt something,
viz. not only that there are big things to be done in
the world, but that America does them, and that
America does more of them than she talks about.

APPENDIX

SINCE the chapter on Magic was written, the publication of Wilhelm Wundt's *Völkerpsychologie*, Vol. II, Part II, has led me to believe that I ought to have laid more stress on the power of the magician, which I mention on pages 74, 85, 86, 87, 88, 89, and less on the savage's recognition of the principle that like produces like. In the stage of human evolution known as Animism, every event which calls for explanation is explained as the doing of some person or conscious agent. When a savage falls ill, his sickness is regarded as the work of some ill-disposed person, whose power cannot be doubted — for it is manifest in the sickness it has caused — and whose power is as mysterious as it is indubitable. That power is what a savage means by magic; and the persons believed to possess it are magicians. It is the business of the sick savage's friends to find out who is causing his sickness. Their suspicion may fall on any one whose appearance or behaviour is suspicious or mysterious; and the person suspected comes to be regarded as a witch or magician, from the very fact that he is suspected. Such persons have the power of witchcraft or magic, because they are believed to have the power: *possunt quia posse videntur.* Not only are they believed to possess the power; they come to believe, themselves, that they possess it. They believe that, possessing it, they have but to exercise it. The Australian magician has but to "point" his stick, and, in the belief both of himself and of every one concerned, the victim will fall. All over the world the witch has but to stab the image she has drawn or made, and the person portrayed will feel the wound. In this proceeding, the image is like the person, and the blow delivered is like the blow which the victim is to feel. It is open to us, therefore, to say that, in this typical case of "imitative" or "mimetic" magic, like is believed to produce like. And on pages 75–77, and elsewhere, above, I have taken that position. But I would now add two qualifications. The first is, as already intimated, that, though stabbing an effigy is like stabbing the victim, it is only a magician or witch that has the power thus to inflict wounds, sickness, or death: the services of the magician or witch are employed for no other reason than that the ordinary person has not the power, even by the aid of the rite, to cause the effect. The second qualification is that, whereas we distinguish between the categories of likeness and identity, the savage makes but little distinction. To us it is evident that stabbing the image is only like stabbing the victim; but to the believer in magic, stabbing the image is the same thing as stabbing the victim; and in his belief, as the waxen image melts, so the victim withers away.

It would, therefore, be more precise and more correct to say (page 74, above) that eating tiger to make you bold points rather to a confusion, in the savage's mind, of the categories of likeness and identity, than to a conscious recognition of the principle that like produces like: as you eat tiger's flesh, so you become bold with the tiger's boldness. The spirit of the tiger enters you. But no magic is necessary to enable you to make the meal: any one can eat tiger. The belief that so the tiger's spirit will enter you is a piece of Animism; but it is not therefore a piece of magic.

BIBLIOGRAPHY

ABT, A. Die Apologie des Apuleius von Madaura und die antike Zauberei. Giessen. 1908.

ALVIELLA, G. Origin and Growth of the Conception of God. London. 1892.

BASTIAN, A. Allerlei aus Volks- und Menschenkunde. Berlin. 1888.

BOUSSET, W. What is Religion? (E. T.). London. 1907.

DAVIES, T. W. Magic, Divination, and Demonology. Leipzig. 1898.

ELLIS, A. B. The Ewe-speaking Peoples of the Slave Coast. London. 1890. The Tshi-speaking Peoples of the Gold Coast. London. 1887. The Yoruba-speaking Peoples of the Slave Coast. London. 1894.

FAHZ, L. De poetarum Romanorum doctrina magica. Giessen. 1904.

FARNELL, L. R. The Place of the Sonder-Götter in Greek Polytheism, in Anthropological Essays. Oxford. 1907.

FRAZER, J. G. Adonis, Attis, Osiris. London. 1905. The Golden Bough. London. 1900. Lectures on the Early History of the Kingship. London. 1905.

GRANGER, F. The Worship of the Romans. London. 1895.

HADDON, H. C. Magic and Fetishism. London. 1906.

HARRISON, J. E. Prolegomena to the Study of Greek Religion. Cambridge. 1903.

HARTLAND, E. S. The Legend of Perseus. London. 1895.

HOBHOUSE, L. T. Morals in Evolution. London. 1906.

HÖFFDING, H. Philosophy of Religion (E. T.). London. 1906.

HOLLIS. The Masai. Oxford. 1905.

HOWITT, A. W.   The Native Tribes of South East Australia.
London. 1904.

HUBERT, H. Magia. In Daremberg Saglio's Dictionnaire
des Antiquités. Paris. 1904.

HUBERT, H. & MAUSS, M. Théorie générale de la magie.
L'Année Sociologique. Paris. 1904. La Nature et la
fonction du sacrifice. L'Année Sociologique. Paris.
1899.

HUVELIN, P. Magie et droit individuel. L'Année Sociologique. Paris. 1907.

ILLINGWORTH, J. R. Personality: Human and Divine. London. 1894.

JEVONS, F. B. The Definition of Magic. Sociological Re-
view for April, 1908. London. The Evolution of the
Religious Consciousness. In Pan-Anglican Papers.
London. 1908. Introduction to the History of Religion.
London. 1896. Magic. In Proceedings of the Inter-
national Congress for the History of Religions. 1908.

LANG, A. Custom and Myth. London. 1893. Magic and
Religion. London. 1901. The Making of Religion.
London. 1898. Modern Mythology. London. 1897.
Myth, Ritual, and Religion. London. 1887.

LENORMANT, F. Chaldean Magic (E. T.). London. 1877.

MACCULLOUGH, J. A. Comparative Theology. London.
1902.

MARETT, R. R. Is Taboo a Negative Magic? In Anthropological Essays. Oxford. 1907.

MAUSS, M. Des Sociétés Eskimos. L'Année Sociologique.
Paris. 1906.

MÜLLER, J. G. Geschichte der amerikanischen Urreligionen.
Basel. 1855.

NASSAU, R. H. Fetichism in West Africa. London. 1904.

PARKER, K. L. The Euahlayi Tribe. London. 1905.

PAYNE, E. J. History of the New World called America. Oxford. 1892.

REINACH, S. Cultes, Mythes, et Religions. Paris. 1905. Reports of the Cambridge Anthropological Expedition to Torres Straits. Cambridge (England). 1908.

RHYS DAVIDS, T. W. Origin and Growth of Religion. London. 1891.

RUHL, L. De Mortuorum indicio. Giessen. 1903.

SCHMIDT, H. Veteres Philosophi quomodo indicaverint de precibus. Giessen. 1907.

SCHRADER, O. Reallexikon der indogermanischen Altertümer. Strassburg. 1901.

SKEAT, W. W. Malay Magic. London. 1900.

SMITH, W. R. Religion of the Semites. London. 1894.

SPENCE, L. The Mythologies of Ancient Mexico and Peru. London. 1907.

SPENCER & GILLEN. The Native Tribes of Central Australia. London. 1899. The Northern Tribes of Central Australia. London. 1904.

TYLOR, E. B. Primitive Culture. London. 1873.

WAITZ, T. Anthropologie der Naturvölker. Leipzig. 1864.

WEBSTER, H. Primitive Secret Societies. London. 1908.

WESTERMARCK, E. The Origin and Development of the Moral Ideas. London. 1906.

WUNDT, W. Völkerpsychologie. Leipzig. 1904-1907.

INDEX

Ghosts, 38, 42.
Gift-theory of sacrifice, 206.
God, worshipped by community, 91, 98; a supreme being, 168; etymology of the word, 133, 134; a personal power, 136, 137; correlative to a community, 137.
Gods and worshippers, 53; and fetichism, 110; made and broken, 110; personal, 121; "departmental," 129; their personality, 130, 131; and the good of the community, 123; and fetiches, 124; are the powers that care for the welfare of the community, 126, 172; and spirits, 128; "of a moment," 128, 136; their proper names, 131; worshipped by a community, 134; and the desires of their worshippers, 134; not evolved from fetiches, 135; promote the community's good, 135, 137, 167; and prayer, 140, 147, 148; and morality, 169; of a community identified with the community, 177; as ethical powers, 215; punish transgression, 220.
Gold Coast, prayer, 143.
Golden Age, 25.
Good, the, 140; and the gods, 137.
Gotama, 64.
Gott, and *giessen*, 134.
Grace, 259.
Gratitude, 181.
Great Spirit, the, 143.
Guardian spirits, 111.
Guinea, 197.

Haddon, Dr., 83, 91, 100, 101, 106, 107, 117, 118, 124, 129, 130, 132, 133.
Hades, 58.

Hallucinations, 38.
Happiness, 240.
Hartford Theological Seminary, 1, 22, 106.
Harvest, prayers and sacrifice, 180 ff.
Harvest communion, 188, 189.
Harvest customs, 192, 198, 203.
Harvest supper, 195 ff., 200; its sacramental character, 197.
Health, and disease, 138.
Heaven, kingdom of, 252, 262.
Hebrew prophets, 207, 209.
Hebrews, 54.
Hegel, 213.
Hindoo Koosh, 194.
Historic science, has the historic order for its object, 11; but does not therefore deny that its facts may have value other than truth value, 11.
History, of art and literature, 8; of religion, 253, 263.
Ho dirge, 47.
Hobhouse, L. T., 211, 214–216, 222, 223, 226–229, 230, 237.
Höffding, H., 44, 166, 173, 254; on fetichism, 106, 114, 115, 121, 124, 128–130, 133–137; on antinomy of religious feeling, 174; and morality, 211, 214–216, 219, 220, 237.
Hollis, Mr., 143 ff.
Homer, 16, 17.
Homœopathic magic, 80, 85, 93.
Homogeneous, the, 23, 24.
Howitt, Mr., 190.
Hu, hula, 134.
Humanitarianism, 214, 215, 236, 244, 246, 247; and morality, 221.
Humanity, 213; its evolution, 244.
Husband, 98.

Ideals, a matter of the will, 13.
Idols, 193.

Other Valuable Books for Students of Ethnology

By FRIEDERICH RATZEL
History of Mankind
Richly illustrated. 3 vols. 8vo. Each, $4.00 net; by mail, $4.32

By CHARLES PICKERING
History of the Races of Man
$1.50 net; by mail, $1.63

By JEROME DOWD
The Negro Races. Vol. I.
$2.50 net; by mail, $2.68

By A. G. LEONARD
The Lower Niger and its Tributaries
8vo. $4.00 net; by mail, $4.20

By DUDLEY KIDD
Kafir Socialism and the Dawn of Individualism
8vo. $2.75 net; by mail, $2.92

The Essential Kafir. With 100 plates from photographs.
8vo. $6.00 net; expressage extra

Savage Childhood. A Study of Kafir Children. Profusely
illustrated from photographs. 8vo. $3.50 net; by mail, $3.66

By R. E. DENNETT
At the Back of the Black Man's Mind; or, Notes on the
Kingly Office in West Africa
Illustrated. 8vo. $3.25 net; by mail, $3.42

By G. W. STOW
Native Races of South Africa
8vo. $6.50 net; expressage extra

By B. SPENCER AND F. J. GILLEN
Native Tribes of Central Australia
$6.50 net; by mail, $6.80

Northern Tribes of Central Australia
$6.50 net; by mail, $6.80

By A. W. HOWITT
Native Tribes of Southeast Australia
$6.50 net; by mail, $6.80

By W. W. SKEAT AND C. O. BLAGDEN
Pagan Races of the Malay Peninsula. Profusely illustrated
from special photographs. 2 vols. 8vo. $13.00 net; by mail, $13.54

PUBLISHED BY

THE MACMILLAN COMPANY
64-66 FIFTH AVENUE, NEW YORK

Studies of Religion
By H. FIELDING HALL

The Soul of a People
Fourth Reprinting of a Fourth Edition
Cloth, 8vo, $3.00 net

An account of observations among the Burmese, before and after the War of Annexation, through which the faith of the people revealed itself.

A People at School
Cloth, 8vo, $3.00 net

It corresponds to the earlier book as the inner life of the feelings, emotions, and ideals is related to the outer life of success and failure, of progress and retrogression, judged as nations judge each other. It treats of the Burmese before annexation and of the ways in which it has affected them.

The Hearts of Men
Cloth, 8vo, $3.00 net

This is a book not of one religion, or several religions, but of religion, treated with the delightful lucidity of the East. There is something very appealing in the whole spirit of this man who seeks for light, a gentleness that is restful, an utter absence of bitterness even where there must be condemnation, a great patience and serenity in that religion which is "the music of the infinite echoed from the hearts of men."

The Inward Light
Cloth, 8vo, $1.75 net; by mail, $1.86

"An enchanting book . . . vital with human interest." — *New York Tribune.*

"Its publication is an event, because it expresses in a new and original form what even the most sceptical cannot but admit to be a rational and beautiful outlook on life." — *North American Review.*

PUBLISHED BY

THE MACMILLAN COMPANY
64-66 FIFTH AVENUE, NEW YORK

The Philosophy of the Christian Religion

By ANDREW MARTIN FAIRBAIRN, Principal of Mansfield College, Oxford, author of "Christ in Modern Theology," "Studies in the Philosophy of Religion."

Cloth, 8vo, xxviii + 583 pages, $3.50 net

"This work is one of the strongest and best published within the last ten years in English in the department commonly known as Apologetics. Its primary object is twofold: first, to explain religion through nature and man, conceiving of it as a joint product of the mind within man and of the nature around him. . . . The second part of the author's design is to construe Christianity through religion, to explain its origin and nature, and indicate its distinctive ideas. . . . This is a book, not simply to be read for the interest of its topic, but to be studied with care and enjoyed as a rare contribution to the philosophy of religion . . .; the work of a master mind." — *The Interior*, Chicago.

"The most important book of its kind that has appeared for years. Dr. Fairbairn is unquestionably one of the most masterful thinkers of the time. . . . He is at the same time intensely modern. He understands exceptionally well the points at which the most vital problems in present day thought have arrived. And so he discerns keenly the points where the fundamental questions of philosophy, science, and religion meet." — *Chicago Tribune*.

The Philosophical Basis of Religion

By JOHN WATSON, M.A., LL.D., Professor of Moral Philosophy in Queen's University, Kingston, Canada.

Cloth, 8vo, xxvi + 485 pages, $3.00 net

"These lectures, six of which were recently given in Brooklyn, and eight others which are critical studies in the historical evolution of religious thought, eminently deserve the attention of those who agree with their author that 'nothing short of a complete revision of theological ideas can bring permanent satisfaction to our highly reflective age.'" — *The Outlook*.

PUBLISHED BY

THE MACMILLAN COMPANY

64-66 FIFTH AVENUE, NEW YORK

1474428R00168

Printed in Germany
by Amazon Distribution
GmbH, Leipzig